FRANCES T. BOURNE
JACARANDA PUBLIC LIBRARY

4143 WOODMERE PARK BLVD.
VENICE, FL 34293

Timothy O'Grady was born in Chicago and has lived in Ireland, London, Spain and Poland. He went to Las Vegas after receiving a fellowship from the Black Mountain Institute and stayed on for another year to teach. That is when he met the 'children of Las Vegas' whose stories appear in this book. He is the author of three novels, *Motherland, I Could Read the Sky* and *Light*, and three works of non-fiction, *Curious Journey, On Golf* and, most recently, *Divine Magnetic Lands. Children of Las Vegas* is his second collaboration with photographer Steve Pyke.

Steve Pyke is considered one of the leading portrait photographers in the world. His work, including the series *Philosophers* and *Astronauts*, has been exhibited worldwide. He has published nine books, and for the past thirty-five years he has worked consistently on a series collecting the Faces of Our Time. In 2004 Steve received the MBE in the Queen's New Year Honours list for his services to the Arts, and in 2006 he was made a Friend of the Royal Photographic Society.

31969026034057

CHILDREN OF
LAS VEGAS

TIMOTHY O'GRADY

WITH PHOTOGRAPHS BY STEVE PYKE

unbound

FRANCES T. BOURNE
JACARANDA PUBLIC LIBRARY
4143 WOODMERE PARK BLVD.
VENICE, FL 34293

This edition first published in 2016

Unbound
6th Floor Mutual House, 70 Conduit Street, London W1S 2GF
www.unbound.co.uk

All rights reserved

Text © Timothy O'Grady, 2016
Images © Steve Pyke, 2016

The rights of Timothy O'Grady and Steve Pyke to be identified as the
authors of this work has been asserted in accordance with Section 77 of
the Copyright, Designs and Patents Act 1988. No part of this publication may
be copied, reproduced, stored in a retrieval system, or transmitted, in any
form or by any means without the prior permission of the publisher, nor
be otherwise circulated in any form of binding or cover other than that in
which it is published and without a similar condition being imposed
on the subsequent purchaser.

While every effort has been made to trace the owners of copyright
material reproduced herein, the publisher would like to apologise
for any omissions and will be pleased to incorporate missing
acknowledgments in any further editions.

Text Design by Carrdesignstudio.com

A CIP record for this book is available from the British Library

ISBN 978-1-78352-250-7 (trade hbk)
ISBN 978-1-78352-251-4 (ebook)
ISBN 978-1-78352-284-2 (limited edition)

Printed in Great Britain by Clays Ltd, St Ives Plc

1 3 5 7 9 8 6 4 2

For Agata and Aleksandra Jacunska

For it is...a shimmering mirage
of riches and mystery and death.

Richard E. Lingenfelter

Dear Reader,

The book you are holding came about in a rather different way to most others. It was funded directly by readers through a new website: Unbound. Unbound is the creation of three writers. We started the company because we believed there had to be a better deal for both writers and readers. On the Unbound website, authors share the ideas for the books they want to write directly with readers. If enough of you support the book by pledging for it in advance, we produce a beautifully bound special subscribers' edition and distribute a regular edition and e-book wherever books are sold, in shops and online.

This new way of publishing is actually a very old idea (Samuel Johnson funded his dictionary this way). We're just using the internet to build each writer a network of patrons. Here, at the back of this book, you'll find the names of all the people who made it happen.

Publishing in this way means readers are no longer just passive consumers of the books they buy, and authors are free to write the books they really want. They get a much fairer return too – half the profits their books generate, rather than a tiny percentage of the cover price.

If you're not yet a subscriber, we hope that you'll want to join our publishing revolution and have your name listed in one of our books in the future. To get you started, here is a £5 discount on your first pledge. Just visit unbound.com, make your pledge and type **lasvegas** in the promo code box when you check out.

Thank you for your support,

Dan, Justin and John
Founders, Unbound

PROLOGUE

I lived in Las Vegas for two years. It was among the last places I expected to be at that stage of my life, but there I was. I was offered a fellowship, and then stayed on to teach. We bought an old gold Mazda that had been bleached and blistered by the sun and rented an apartment beside a golf course in Henderson. From the little balcony I watched the unceasing chain of planes bringing tourists to the Strip. 'The jewel box,' a great-grandmother once said of it to a small boy. You will meet them both later in these pages. At night you can see the Strip from anywhere in the valley if you are pointed in the right direction. It's like a small galaxy throbbing on the desert floor. Las Vegas may like to take away your sense of time and space, but it will always remind you of what you are there for.

I once imagined that I would like to visit Las Vegas more than anywhere else on earth. It was the destination I chose when asked to write a school paper on what would be my favourite vacation. I was fourteen years old and had no idea of what I might do there. But its aura was enough. Perhaps I thought the choice would surprise, that I would gain some position over other boys who would write of the Super Bowl or fishing in Wisconsin or museums in Madrid. I would say that was my aim. It was still a little before the time when a sweaty Elvis was doing karate chops in his rhinestone spacesuits. It was still cool, at least by reputation. It was our version of the Côte d'Azur. The images came down the line to us on television. There were the long cars with the high fins, the winking doormen, the Sammy Davis Jr suits. Vegas was louche and urban and knowing. People there walked on the edge and seemed at ease with it. They laughed at how extravagantly frivolous they could be with their money or their reputations. Even the women were rakish. You could see it glinting somewhere in their diamantine eyes as they sat around the roulette tables. As I later heard Simone de Beauvoir said of it: 'No bourgeoisie, no bourgeois morality.'

It held no allure for me by the time I got there four decades later, but I watched it nevertheless. It asks you to, and it's hard to refuse. I walked and drove and talked and sat on our little balcony trying to figure it out, not only the Strip, but the city itself that spread through the valley in low lines and pale colours out to the horizon. It's a global star. It flashes in the eyes. Mention it anywhere and you will get a response – bedazzlement, envy, a raising of the brow, an avuncular warning. People you know want your report on it if you're right there in the front row.

But I couldn't catch it. Not after a month, not even after a year. It seemed always to be receding, like something slipping away in

a tide. Houses are behind walls, their windows opaque. Drivers
way above you are screened by tinted glass in SUVs the size of
fire trucks. Almost no one walks. Buildings seem to take a step
backwards behind gigantic parking lots or entrance halls just as
you feel you are getting near them. If you open a door to a bar
you meet perpetual night behind blackened windows. The faces
looking up from the poker machines are like ramparts. There is
no focal point, no main square or central business district with
office workers walking around in shirtsleeves on their breaks, no
Luxembourg Gardens or Central Park, just this glittering trinket
that can be seen from space, its surface dazzle and electronic
colour leading you deeper and deeper into caverns that are only
more surface. Who did it belong to? Not the people I saw in the
supermarket. In the centre the visitors are the aristocracy, the
citizens their vassals.

We didn't meet many visitors, or citizens. There were three
pools and a hundred and something units in our development,
but little stirred there. In two years we never saw our downstairs
neighbours, but there was life there, we could see, for the
blue-grey light of their television flickered against their perma-
nently drawn blinds. You'd hear the hum of air conditioners,
the killing of engines, see the shadow of someone coming
home late thrown hugely onto a wall by a ground light. But
faces were rare. The only one I saw with any regularity was a
slender, middle-aged man I could see going to work from our
bedroom window, his hair oiled, his white shirt gartered high
on the sleeves for dealing cards, his expression sour. Around us,
we supposed, were the homes, or former homes, of the retired,
the repossessed, the winter sojourners, the cocktail shakers,

towel haulers and wheel spinners. We just couldn't see them, and didn't understand why. Where was everybody in what had been until recently America's fastest growing city? Why did everything seem so far away?

Sometimes in the day's last light we walked around the golf course, whose eleventh tee was just below our balcony. If you walk the streets you have for the most part walls for company. Here along the fairways it was all backyards – the backyards of houses small and large, the backyards of mansions built in the style of mausoleums. There wasn't a thing in any of them that could tell you if anyone lived in them – no towel or toy or tennis racquet. The windows were blank. They seemed screened with a kind of mesh that was the colour of the desert. It was like walking into a room full of people with their eyes and mouths sewn shut. It was like a Twilight Zone episode without a plot.

Steve Wynn opened the Mirage ten years before we arrived. He raised $604 million in New York, built the largest casino resort in the world and installed luxury fittings throughout, a twenty-thousand-gallon tank with pygmy sharks and stingrays in it, an ecologically precise rainforest on the casino floor and a giant volcano in the forecourt that went off every fifteen minutes. Four thousand service workers were employed to run it.

It was a large bet and it paid out. Two hundred thousand people came to the opening. The city entered a new boom time. The resorts themselves, rather than the gambling halls and shows, were now the attraction. Old hotels, even the Desert Inn, were blown up, and vast new Disneyesque ones like Excalibur, Treasure Island, the MGM Grand and others alluding to Venice, Paris, New York and ancient Egypt were built. There was soon a higher hotel-room count on the corner of Las Vegas Boulevard and Flamingo than in the whole of San Francisco. There were by then casinos in twenty-three states, but Las Vegas kept growing, for Americans were spending nearly the same cut of the gross national product on gambling as on groceries. Thirty-five million people came every year, more than to Mecca. You could make $70,000 parking cars or dealing cards and in one step go from a trailer park to a middle-class home. A great new migration took place. Among those who came were the parents of some of the people whose stories are in this book.

In our second year I began to teach. The boom was over by then. You could see halted construction projects all over the city, including some in the heart of the Strip. The university was considering deleting Philosophy, and a few other departments. A tent city on the edge of downtown had just been cleared. Las Vegas had become the hardest city of its size to find work in and also led in home foreclosures.

I'd already taught a little, in England, Poland, on the east coast of the United States. The students in Las Vegas were different. I asked a class of twenty-six how many worked and found that all but one did, full time, mostly in casinos. One occasionally missed class because of a conflict with his shift as a stripper. Some worked through the night, or did double shifts at weekends. All had full course loads. When did they read, or write essays? I found too that they carried debts, some up around $40,000, for being educated in a state university. They lived with their parents, they were legally considered dependants. But it seemed that economically they were on their own. Sometimes good students turned in flimsy work and if I asked them about it they said they knew, they were sorry, they'd do it again if I'd give them the chance. It was just that they were exhausted.

One day they showed up to my class with not a single one having read the story I'd assigned. They couldn't afford the textbook, they said, and this particular story wasn't anywhere online. It was a California story about how a mother's expectations about her daughter drove both of them mad. I told them the plot and asked them what they thought.

'Our parents want us to get good grades so we'll keep our scholarships and they won't be asked to pay for anything,' said a young man with an unusual degree of bitterness, especially for him.

'They go through our pockets and steal our money,' said a young woman beside him.

I thought I'd misheard and asked her to repeat what she'd said.

'They're still drunk when they wake up,' said another. 'I have to get them to work and my brothers and sisters fed and to school.'

'My mom stole my sister's wedding money,' said someone in the front row.

We had an hour and a quarter and I let it run. It seemed to feed on its own momentum, like testimonials of revelation in a church. They spoke of routinely losing their homes, of raising themselves, of having their identities stolen in credit-card frauds committed by their parents. There were overdoses, desert shoot-outs, suicides. I'd never heard anything like that in a single room. Nearly everyone spoke. The pitch was at its highest when the class ended. It was as if a jail door had opened for a time.

Editors send writers out to catch Las Vegas, as if it were a concept. The people that create the identity of the city also think of it that way. It changes often, it reinvents itself because it has to, but this is less a process of development than a succession of images, a new kind of girl popping up out of the cake. The rest of the city, where the citizens live, is out of focus, not quite there. Most of the people who think at all about Las Vegas think of it this way. A student told me that when she went to Philadelphia for a conference as a representative of her high school council she was asked if she lived in a hotel and if there were any schools in her city. I tried to write about Las Vegas too, but all I could really see when I looked at it were walls and distance and questions I had no answers to.

If anything could get me closer, I thought, it would be my students. This strange celebrity of a city had been happening to them all their lives. They'd watched it in a way that adults or visitors or, of course, writers, could not. I wanted to hear all that they had to say, and thought others should too.

The next time I had a class I asked a few of them if they'd be willing to be interviewed, named and photographed for a piece of journalism about their city. I assumed they'd refuse. How could they not? It would lay bare not only themselves, but their families. Each of them said they would do it, however. They seemed to have a need to do so. I was led by the people I'd met to some others – a businessman, a homeless woman, a policeman, a casino child. A few hesitated. A few declined in the end. But the rest, like my students, seemed to have a need to testify and would live with what it might cost them. In the end I had ten, but if I'd kept looking I'd have had hundreds more.

One by one they came to our apartment beside the golf course and talked to me. I called Steve Pyke and he flew in from New York to photograph them. They all grew up in Las Vegas. Theirs are not the only kinds of stories about growing up there, but the things that happened to them happen not only everywhere in the city, as they told me, but also because of it. Anyone who'd like to know need only ask.

Why'd they call it that? You'd think
they wouldn't want people to know.

Tourist, looking at the Mirage

Don't worry that children never
listen to you.
Worry that they are always watching you.

Robert Fulghum

SHELBY SULLIVAN

Student

We were happy, until we weren't. I had the ideal childhood. We had our house, there were kids to play with. It was a good neighbourhood then. My dad was a chef at Treasure Island and my mom was a cashier at the Mirage, where she still is. They met when they were living at the same apartment complex downtown. They loved it here. Then one thing happened, and another, and another. It all just went downhill so fast.

My dad drank. I wasn't aware of that for a long time. I guess I was too young to tell. We had this little wishing-well barbecue pit in the backyard. We kept a board over it and when we took it off one day we found all these empty bottles my dad had put in there. He drank an eight-pack of beer before going to work one day and they fired him. That was the start, I think. Then my aunt moved in and all these arguments started. My mom and her would argue over something like towels. 'You took my dish rag!' It would start like that and escalate until my mom would say, 'Get out of my house!' Then my aunt would say, 'Oh yes, this is yours and this and this and this. Everything is yours!' My mom would get mad at my dad if he didn't step in, but then if he did and took her side she'd be mad that he was attacking her sister. My parents also argued about money. She had six different credit cards running up debt at the same time. She bought things, she gambled. She said she deserved it because she supported everyone else when my dad was out of work and she was everybody's slave. My aunt and her daughter would argue about who was a worse mother. It's a fiasco. My family has this thing where if something is wrong you have to out-scream the other person and bring up whatever you can from what's happened before to hurt them.

I think I was eleven when my aunt moved in with us. She lived with her daughter for a while, but got kicked out. My grandparents kicked her out too. She filled up their house with this junk she collects. They couldn't cope. My mom took her in then. My aunt was kind of wild when she was young. She used to go to work at a casino and then go out to bars. When my cousin was little she had the numbers of the bars her mom went to and knew all the bartenders' names and their shifts. She had quite a few boyfriends – the alcoholic she had my cousin with and a very controlling and rich Hispanic man, among others. She was engaged to a drug addict who told her he was a pilot. She still wound up paying for his flying lessons later. They got in an argument once and he ran over her with his car. She doesn't go to bars now. She takes meth, works part-time as a dealer at Boulder Station and gambles. She comes home with nothing, just blows her whole paycheque. And she still collects junk. She drives around looking for it and waits outside storage places so she can collect stuff people throw out.

After she moved in she and my mom started going to Sam's Town casino on Boulder Highway. It was my grandparents' favourite. My mom played bingo and then slots and my aunt played tables and slots. When my grandparents and aunt would leave my mom would stay on. She'd say she'd be along soon but she didn't come and when they went back the next day she'd still be sitting there. She'd have taken out all the money she could get on her A.T.M. and credit cards.

Maybe you can't pin everything on one thing, one person especially. Maybe it's not fair. But it's hard not to blame my aunt for all the bad things that happened. I remember my mom's warmth. She took my aunt in because she was always such a caring, family-oriented type of person. The change was so stark. She snaps, she's defensive, she thinks everyone's out to get her. My dad went to A.A. after she gave him an ultimatum and as he got better she got worse. She gets in these terrible fights with my aunt. My aunt has ripped chunks of her hair out of her head and my mom has hit my aunt so hard her false tooth has fallen out. It happens right in front of us. I've been hit trying to break it up.

I found my mom's straws and razor blades when I was in eighth grade. She snorts meth. I don't know when she started, but it was my aunt who brought it here. She'll go into the bathroom and turn on the faucet for thirty minutes and then deny she was doing it. Or else she'll say she does it to lose weight or because she has to stay up and clean the house. You can hear her at night when she's high, cleaning and doing laundry. One time I came home and she and my aunt were screaming about who'd used the last of it. My mom said, 'I wouldn't have to do it if I didn't have to clean up after my lazy children.' So it's our fault. She gets nosebleeds. Soon her septum will deviate.

I know she's miserable. She doesn't see anybody, or even want to. She just stays in her room and only comes out to go to work. She views the world in such a skewed way. We drove her all the way back to La Crosse, Wisconsin, where she was born, for her fiftieth birthday and she stood outside the house, yelling, 'All I want for my birthday is a gun so I can shoot myself.' Well, now we have one because we had a break-in. She told my grandma that she has a loaded gun and that there's no reason for her to be here because my brother and I are old enough to look after ourselves now. One day we'll come home and she won't be there, she says. That, or she'll kill my aunt.

Her and me were so close when I was little. I went to her for everything, then she wasn't there. Even if she is there it's not her. It's a different person from the one I knew. It's like living with a stranger. That's what hurts me the most. She's so close, right next to me, and I want her so bad but…she's not there.

When I was in eighth or ninth grade I started self-mutilating. It wasn't even until after I'd stopped for a while that anyone noticed. I think at first I wanted to see if anyone would notice, then I kind of got used to doing it. Everything was changing and I couldn't fix it. When they'd argue I started to scratch, scratch until the skin broke, but then I started to get razor blades. Somehow it made me feel a little better. It was something I could control. I'd cut my legs in places where I could hide it. One time I left the house and was walking along the street. A neighbour had one of those mailboxes with the little red flag sticking up. I broke that off and used it to cut myself. That left a pretty decent scar.

I got out of cutting because of my best friend. If I felt like I was losing it she'd come right over in her car and we'd just drive and drive along the freeway without thinking of where we were going until I felt all right. I basically lived with her family through my senior year in high school. Her mom calls me her middle child. They really saved me. There was just so much poison in my house. When my mom found out about the cutting she said, 'You're sick. You're what's wrong with this family. You need help.' She just tears me down. She says I'm overweight, unattractive, that I'll never find a boyfriend.

The whole city does that to you. You see those pictures of women and think if you don't fit that mould you're not what people want. Even the family shows have scantily clad women in them. They're the role models. The way men treat us is disgusting. People I hang out with even do it. They call us 'skanks', 'bitches', 'sluts'. It's like we're not people, we're just some degraded sub-section.

I started drinking after I stopped cutting. I drank Captain Morgan, or my personal favourite, Southern Comfort. I'd go over to this house belonging to friends of my brother and we'd drink shots around the table. I'd pass out sometimes. Once I fell down and broke two of my teeth. My friend and I figured out that during our first semester at college we were only sober seven days. They dealt weed from that house. Strangers would arrive at all hours. One of them kept a gun under his bed. Everything was very shady there, very negative. Like home. I've slowed down a lot now, though. I like a clear head. I got scared too because I didn't want to be an alcoholic like my dad. 'I can't tell you not to, because I was doing the same thing,' he said, but I could see that for the first time he was disappointed in me. I've been lucky, though. I've had help. I don't know what would have happened if I didn't. My friend made me realize that just because I couldn't find stability at home didn't mean I couldn't find it somewhere else. I had a wonderful teacher who gave me the compliments my mother wasn't able to. That made school a kind of refuge. I was an honours student. My brother's been very good, too. Maybe he didn't get the full impact of it. He had sports and I kind of protected him a little when he was younger. Now we look after each other when we can. It's hard to work full time as I do and also go to school and then come home to all that tension, but he and I just got Netflix and we tune out together with that.

I think my aunt was happy once. She was a cocktail waitress. She looked for fun everywhere. She used to clean her bathroom with a toothbrush and now she dives into dumpsters looking for junk. She was just supposed to be with us for a couple of months, but it's been nine years. Nothing seems to be able to stop it. My dad has given up. I think he feels defeated. My grandma has offered to pay all the costs of getting her out. My brother and I beg my mom to do it, but she won't. She chooses her sister over her kids. I think she wants her nearby because that's where she gets the meth from. Sometimes she puts her foot down and throws her out, but then after a couple of weeks she cracks and my aunt's back again. She always has what my mom needs. I once took a bag of chips from my aunt when she was on the couch and there was a little yellow bag of meth inside. She'll drop one of them on the floor sometimes and I'll look at her to let her know that I know what it is. I don't wish anyone any harm, but I like the times they're not talking because at least then my mom will be clear of the drugs for a while.

We haven't been able to have a family meal since my aunt arrived because her make-up and shoes and bits of junk are on the kitchen table. She's filled four sheds with it out in the backyard. You have to keep to the left in the hallway because one side is full of boxes and storage tubs. My mom has to put her stuff in boxes because if she doesn't my aunt'll think it's hers. She might take it out to the front to wash it down with a hose. That's what she keeps doing with that stuff. One side of my bed is blocked by boxes. It's everywhere. It just spreads. It's like a disease. You can't touch her stuff because she gets mad. She throws things.

Before she came I was into art. I used to design cards for my parents. They loved them. I pictured this happy future where I'd own my own design company and make art. Then everything started to happen. Now I just put as much effort as I can into school so I can get out of here and far, far away to some safe, warm environment that makes sense. I want to live somewhere I'm not ashamed of. I feel like my family is the joke of the town, that I've been dealt the worst hand. I can't bring anyone to my house. I have to ask them to pick me up somewhere down the street. My aunt will be out in front with a do-rag and a missing tooth washing grocery bags. No one knows why. She's dark-skinned from all her time in the sun and she doesn't brush her hair for days. She'll dress properly for work but otherwise her clothes are torn and full of bleach stains. She wears bright pink shoes. I've found her many times passed out on the toilet with a cigarette hanging from her mouth. Once she fell asleep on the couch and spilled a bowl of cereal on herself. She just woke up and brushed it off. The house is a sore thumb. There's just dirt in the front yard and trash cans full of empty soda cans she's supposedly going to cash in one day. They attract bees. You have to run down the path to get away from them. It was a decent house once. Now there's broken junk everywhere, dead plants outside my window. The paint on the house is flaking off because of the chemicals she uses to clean her stuff. There's always water running out of the hose. She won't clean the house but she'll clean her junk for hours. She'll pick rocks out of the dirt and wash them. It's got to the point where I take all this as normal now until I think of other people seeing it, or if I tell them about it. I once told my boss and he was amazed. 'But you're always smiling,' he says. 'I thought life was easy for you. I took you for a spoiled rich kid.'

I'm saving up for a car, and then a place to live. I have to pay for school myself. My dad helped me the first semester with textbooks, but when my mom found out she made me pay her back the $600 he'd given me. She said it was her money. She keeps a chart of my debts to her.

People come to Vegas to blow off steam and then go. But I'm stuck here. When I see the city lights I think of all the parts they don't shine on. I feel like I'm living there, in those parts. The shadows pull you under. There's so much distance between me and the lights.

Shelby Sullivan graduated with a degree in English Literature from UNLV in December 2013 and is in the process of becoming a high school English teacher. In the meantime she continues to work at a Sonic fast-food outlet in Las Vegas. Her aunt was finally evicted from the family house. She also lost her job at the casino. Shelby's mother ceased using drugs and their relationship greatly improved. She would like to live in the east, or perhaps Wisconsin, where her mother is from.

PARADISE

The Strip is not in Las Vegas, but rather in an unincorporated district called Paradise. Creating an enclave was a mob idea, designed to avoid city taxes. I couldn't find out who named it, though, or what they had in mind.

It is a city in which all adjectives are in the superlative – the biggest, the highest, the fastest, the most gallons or roses or megawatts. To use moderate language would be to somehow fail in a civic duty. On Las Vegas's one hundredth birthday a cake was baked that consisted of one hundred and thirty thousand eggs, thirty-six thousand cups of sugar and twenty-four thousand pounds of flour. Mayor Oscar Goodman said, 'People have been asking me, "Why such a big birthday cake?" Well, you're only a hundred years old once, and to have anything less than that would be very un-Vegas. This has to be the biggest, the best, the most exciting, and that's what Vegas is. This is symbolic for us...this perfect birthday cake, the greatest party for the greatest city in the history of the world.'

Las Vegas tells you that it offers you the ultimate ever conceived by human thought, a paradise, tailored to your specifications, at least for as long as your money lasts. What is the nature of this paradise? The late Hal Rothman, an historian at the University of Nevada, said, 'The difference between Venice and the Venetian is that the latter is cleaner, a little less noisy and has all the amenities. So it takes the world the way it is and makes it the way you would have it if you were in charge.' It is, or is billed to be, a fantasy, an escape, a place where play is all, where you can imagine who you would like to be and then actually be it, where you can ease yourself away from thought and act at all times on impulse, where Dionysius prevails over Apollo twenty-four hours per day and you need fear no moral reckoning. It is taken care of. What happens in Vegas stays in Vegas.

Paradise means orchard. Aphrodite gives Paris an apple just as the Hesperides give one to Heracles, for the apple is the means of admittance to the Elysian Fields, the orchard in the west where only heroes can go. All Neolithic and Bronze Age paradises were orchards, just as the paradise in the Bible was, only there the gift of an apple by woman to man was a trick and brought a fall rather than eternal life.

NEVADA STUPAK

Businessman
Son of a casino owner

My dad found a stuntman and offered him a million bucks to jump off the Stratosphere. Highest freefall ever. I got the day off school to watch it. I saw the guy, just a little speck way up on the ledge. He must have been up there for more than twenty minutes, thinking long and hard about it. Then off he went, came sailing down, landed on an air mattress. No problem, just hopped off, walked over to my dad to collect the million dollars. He thought he was made. My dad says, 'Did you read the contract?' The guy goes, 'Yeah, I'm a millionaire!' 'Check again,' says my dad. 'There's a $990,000 landing fee.' The guy was freaking out. He'd risked his life and all he was getting was ten thousand bucks. But what could he do? He's a daredevil, not a businessman. He doesn't read contracts.

That was the Vegas style before the super-chefs, the super-rooms. It was carnival land, Barnum and Bailey, Evel Knievel jumping over buses. Coupons! Two for one! Try your luck! My dad was always making up things – promotional stunts, discount offers, new casino games. He had one deal where you could play tic-tac-toe with a chicken for money. I grew up with that. Acrobats would come over to the house and do flips off the diving board. I used to sit right up on the stage with an Elvis impersonator. His name was Morris. A front-row seat wasn't good enough. I thought he was Elvis. Morris, he was my idol back then.

My dad grew up in gambling. His father ran an illegal craps game on the third floor of a restaurant and bar establishment called the Lotus Club in Pittsburgh. It went on for fifty years. Chester Stupak, he was a big man in Pittsburgh. He knew every cop and politician in town. There was a pool table, dice and a sliding window on the door. I saw it in operation myself. If a competitor opened up my grandfather would go over there and try to bust them. That was my dad's standard. He was pure gambling, blue collar. Steve Wynn came in here with everything premium-brand – marble halls, luxurious carpet, great contemporary art on the walls. My grandfather used to put up a stack of bread, a stack of baloney and a stack of cheese. Anybody got hungry they could make themselves a sandwich. My dad was the same. As far as he was concerned a gambler only wants to look at the table, the chips and the dealer, not at how good the restaurant and art are.

My dad learned the math for gambling from my grandfather. The thing was to get them in and let the probabilities bring you the money. 1.5, that was the number for blackjack. That was the percentage figure for the house advantage. 'Every bet costs you money,' he'd say to me. 'You put $10,000 down on blackjack and it costs you $150.' I couldn't understand it for the longest time. 'But what if you win?' I'd say. 'Doesn't matter, still costs $150.' 'But *how*?' I'd say. 'You've got the extra ten you've just won.' And he'd say, 'The statistical advantage to the house, over time, is $150.' I was thinking in actual situations while he was thinking in mathematical probabilities. Of course anyone can get lucky. The stories of the big winners are the greatest thing for promoting the gaming business. It makes people think they can win, while for the most part gamblers are desperate people who are losing their money because the math runs true. My dad learned that in childhood.

He went off to Australia when he was eighteen with the idea of selling coupons. They were a new thing there. He came back with a new wife and some money. He wanted to be bigger than his dad in gambling, so he chose Vegas. It's the Duel of the Titans all the time here. In little bars, flashy clubs, big casinos, boardrooms, wherever, there's somebody checking the terrain to figure out how to be the most important person in the room. When my dad got here Benny Binion was the bar. Had to be bigger than him. Then Steve Wynn wanted to beat my dad. Then Kirk Kerkorian took Steve Wynn down in a hostile takeover. Steve told me about it himself. He took a call from Kirk in his closet. Kirk says, 'Steve, I just wanted you to hear this from me. I'm going to make an offer on your hotels tomorrow.' Steve says, 'Kirk, you know I'll never sell,' and Kirk goes, 'I know, I know. I just wanted you to hear it from me.' Eight days later the deal was done. Kirk made an offer and the shareholders took it. Wasn't a thing Steve could do about it. Steve calls him and says, 'Why did you do that? You know I built this company from the ground up. My whole life is in this.' And Kirk says, 'But Steve, I had to do it. I couldn't have built all that *myself.*' 'The Smiling Cobra', that's what they called Kirk. The way some of these guys operate now you've got to spend more than you can possibly recoup just to stay in the game.

My dad started with a small property where the Stratosphere is now. He opened a place called Bob Stupak's World Famous Historic Gambling Museum. It was a way of getting an entry-level gaming licence. He changed that into the Million Dollar. He put money all over the walls behind Plexiglass. The whole place was money. It caught fire and my mom and the staff were running around trying to throw all the money into the pool. From there he got a loan from an adventurous banker here named E. Parry Thomas and built a hundred-room hotel called Vegas World. Filled it up with models of spaceships and planets. It started slow, but then he came up with a blackjack variant he called Double Exposure 21 where both the dealer's first two cards are face-up. That drew a lot of people who didn't get the repercussions of the fine print, which said that all ties went to the dealer. That put the house advantage up from 1.5 to 3.5. He paid the whole loan back in six months.

At that point Caesars had been at the top for twenty years. Las Vegas Boulevard and Flamingo, that was the epicentre. Then Steve Wynn raised money from junk bonds and had the nerve to build the Mirage right next to Caesars. Steve had been to the Wharton School of Business. He was smart. He also brought an unprecedented level of class to Vegas. People could see that the Mirage was better than Caesars. My dad started thinking about how he'd trump Steve. We were way over in downtown, far from the action. So he came up with the idea of a huge hotel with the Stratosphere tower way above the rest of the city. 'Instead of being two miles away from the Mirage,' he said, 'I'll make the Mirage two miles away from me.' A poker-playing friend of his put up $550 million, made my dad the chairman of the board and the largest individual shareholder, and he started to build.

We'd lived in a gated community, but then moved over to 6th and Franklin. You could walk to the Stratosphere from there. This is a dirt town, a poor town. I found that out when we moved. Ted Binion lived across from us and Jack was just down the street, but most of the other people around there were bussers, desk clerks, valet parkers, dealers, maintenance men, waitresses. They're my neighbours, your neighbours, everybody's neighbours. A lot of people arrive here as if from the moon. You never learn anything about where they're from. This is a city where a burnt-out case can come and erase his past, start again. And they can do pretty well if nothing pulls them down. All the guys I was talking about before, bar Steve – Benny, Kirk, my dad – they never got out of high school or even into it and they accumulated millions, billions. My dad came out of an illegal gambling room in a steel-mill city and became the chief executive of the third most expensive hotel-resort destination in the history of the world. He ran for mayor. Of course, it's not like that for everybody.

I could never figure out where people were coming from when I was a teenager. They were nice to me because of my dad, or they felt entitled to use me. They borrowed shirts from me, or shoes, then wouldn't give them back. To them it was, like, 'It's not like he *needs* it.' You know what I mean? I could be chasing these things for weeks. All my life I've had these desperate people after me in this twenty-four hour town. I tried to pretend that I didn't have money, but my dad had his name up on the side of a building you could see from everywhere. He bet a million dollars one day on the Super Bowl. The whole town knew about him. I didn't want to stick out, but my first name was Nevada and my second was Stupak. It's not like I could introduce myself as 'Tom' and no one would know. There was just nowhere for me to hide in this town.

My dad brought a lot of misery into the house. There was violence. My sister and I saw it. There was substance abuse, drink. Obviously he wasn't faithful. He made a lot of money and did what he wanted. When he got there it was like he didn't need my mom any more, so he ignored her. One day she just left. She didn't say a word. All we knew was that she wasn't coming home any more, and then about three weeks later we heard she was back in Australia. She couldn't handle it. She came from a town of ten thousand people where her father was the butcher and then she came here and got hit by the Vegas storm. My sister went over to her. I went too after a while. It was too weird for me, putting on a sports jacket and tie to go to a private school in Melbourne when I'd been going around Vegas in Jimmy Z shorts with a Velcro strap, a Gotcha T-shirt and some fancy sneakers. I missed Vegas too much. I'm a casino kid. So I came back.

I lived with my dad and a nanny then. He was never there. He'd call and say, 'I'll be back in ten minutes,' and I wouldn't see him for three weeks. I used to go through his pockets to get by. Sometimes he'd have five or ten grand in there and I'd take a few hundred bucks. He wouldn't miss it, but that was money for a thirteen-year-old kid. Most kids I knew were lucky to have three dollars in their pockets.

I got kicked out of school all the time. I'd talk back to teachers – you know, 'Don't tell me what to do.' It was exciting. I didn't think I had anything to lose. I didn't think I needed an education to earn a living. My dad never went to high school. My mom dropped out. I figured I'd advanced the family educationally just by getting through eleventh grade. And what was it for? My dad owned a casino and bet a million dollars on the Super Bowl. I could go into the Stratosphere and sign for anything I wanted. I was supposed to sweat it out in school just to get a $15 an hour job? Money was irrelevant.

I'd go with friends and hang out at fast-food places and if the cops didn't have anything better to do they'd slap curfew violation tickets on you. I had a bunch of them. One day a judge said he'd put me away if I came up before him again. That didn't really shake me. It was just Juvenile Hall. So I was caught again and brought in front of the same judge. My dad had hired a high-powered attorney but the judge said to me, 'I warned you,' then turned to the guard and said, 'Cuff him.' Juvenile Hall was just behind the court. I thought it was pretty cool when I first saw it – there was a basketball court, a cafeteria. It was like a high school rec room. I thought I'd hang out with the guys there shooting baskets. But that wasn't the programme. They put me in a freezing shower and locked me in a room for two days. All I could do was sit there. The pillow smelled of disinfectant. It got right into the nasal passage and I couldn't get rid of it for days. Finally, through the little window I had, I heard the sound of my mother's car pulling up. She'd moved back to Vegas by then. She had this convertible Mercedes and I could always recognize the sound of the engine. I heard her high heels clicking along on the sidewalk. I'd had way more than enough by then. Another ten minutes would have been a challenge. She asked me what I wanted to do. Going straight home wouldn't have been enough. I needed some fix of something to make me feel good. The Forum shops over at Caesars had just opened. That had to be the global high point of luxury shopping. We went over there and had a meal under this blue kind of Mediterranean sky they'd painted on the ceiling. I just soaked it all up until I calmed down.

Vegas can do that to you. It can make you feel good about life. The polished marble, the Louis Vuitton shops, the chefs and glamour and great entertainment. Where else has there been $20 billion invested in a single street in five years? You just walk up the carpet to these palaces and the doorman opens the door for you, acknowledges you. It's food and oxygen for me. I miss it when I'm away. My uncle got sick and when I went over to Australia to see him my cousins asked me what I wanted to do. 'Let's go over to the Crown Hotel Casino,' I said. I sat there all day. I didn't even gamble. For you maybe it's sitting in your living room sipping a cup of tea. For me it's a casino. I just had to be there.

My parents didn't know what to do with me and didn't have time to figure it out. School wasn't working. They hired an educational consultant and the result was that I was sent to a private school in Italy. It was a therapeutic institution for troubled kids of parents who were rich but didn't want to deal with their kids themselves. It was all right. I was there for twenty-one straight months. I had to learn how to do things I hadn't always done before, like clean up and make my own bed. I came back and kind of stumbled through high school and eventually got a degree in hotel management from a college that had a good programme in Boca Raton, Florida. Sports kind of saved me. I got into volleyball and basketball. It was a release for all the anger or stress or anxiety I'd built up. I could go out on the court and forget about that. It's all on the line in sports. People are watching – your coach, your teammates. You don't want to let them down or embarrass yourself.

My dad was living the dream, he was a king in his domain. But then he had a long fall from grace that started in 1995 when his motorcycle went into the side of a car that had pulled out in front of him. I was on the back. I went sailing over the top of the car and broke my leg, but he went right through it head first. Broke his wrist, pelvis and every bone in his face, lost all his teeth and his sight in the right eye. His head swelled up to something like twice the size and I had to okay a non-F.D.A.-certified drug to treat it. It was astonishing he survived. Most people thought he wouldn't. He got through, but he was never the same. He was well into his fifties, disfigured, seriously damaged both mentally and physically. What does it do to your confidence when you look in the mirror and see this misshapen face? The Stratosphere was under construction at the time of the accident, but by the time it was open he wasn't really fit to run it. He had some bad luck and made some poor decisions. He was probably worth, all told, a couple hundred million. He had offers to buy out his stake in the Stratosphere for $160 million, then ninety, sixty, thirty-eight. His stock had been at $14 and it went right down to zero. He had to walk away from it with nothing. It was the only thing he'd known, he'd been in some piece of property that was his all his adult life, some place he went to every day. And now there was nowhere. He didn't know what to do with his time. There's no doubt he was depressed. Even after he lost the Stratosphere he still had around $30 million in other properties, but he was a high-stakes gambler. He'd make these wild bets like the one on the Super Bowl. The math ran true. Thirteen years after the accident he died alone, and broke.

I didn't used to sit around thinking, 'The Stratosphere is going to be mine. I'm going to change the name on the sign one day from Bob to Nevada.' I always knew it was his deal. But I didn't necessarily think it was *not* going to be mine either. Know what I mean? There's a friend of mine here in town. His dad went to jail for selling pot and his mom's a cocktail waitress. All his life he's lived in apartments at the lowest level. For him, all he could do was go up. He was determined to succeed. He doesn't drink, he doesn't do drugs, he's very successful in real estate. Whatever he was going to do he was going to rise above where he'd come from. But with me, my dad was such a big deal, people were always going, 'You're in, you're gonna have this and that.' I tried to distance myself a little. I tried to weather the storm and all the dust he was kicking up, but I have to say, when all the money went, I wasn't entirely prepared. I came back from college and got an intern job as a craps dealer at the El Cortez. I figured my grandfather and dad had done it. I had no idea how miserable it would be. I went on to being a casino host for high-end players. I was at the Hard Rock, and Caesars. That involved getting them in, keeping them there, making them feel good, issuing their complimentaries. In this town how much you gamble dictates who you are – what type of room you get, the seats you get at the prize fights and shows, who acknowledges you and who doesn't, whether or not you're introduced to the celebrities in the show rooms. I worked on that for the casino. I also had to deal with their requests for extra credit. You eat a lot of shit with these people. They're high demand. They're negotiators by trade and they want to get every inch out of you, just on principle, just for fun. They were people who made it in property, mortgages, things like flooring. They could be New York traders, IPO experts. There were pimps, drug dealers, conmen with years of jail time. But green is green. Vegas isn't picky. They don't care how you get it, as long as you lose it. I had this one guy in the high-limit room, drunk, doing cocaine, spitting on me, demanding an increase in his credit line at 5.30 in the morning and screaming at me, 'I'm gonna buy this fuckin' casino and the first thing I'm gonna fuckin' do is *fire* you. Got it?' I need that for two hundred and fifty bucks a day? I brought in a million dollars in business swallowing stuff from assholes like that. The management called me in, congratulated me, made a little ceremony of handing me an envelope with a bonus cheque in it. Guess what it was for? $828.

Then on top of that you've got the attitudes of the people you're working with. Look carefully and you'll see the casino workers walking the floor talking out of the sides of their mouths. They're saying, 'Fuck this guy, he's an asshole. Fuck that one, he won a million bucks and all he tipped me was a fuckin' hundred.' These people see all kinds of human vileness and they get infected. Some of them look for any chance to rob the casino. They've got their excuse right there – 'It's not like they *need* it.' And where was the road upwards for me? How do I get past all those strata of the hierarchy? And even if you get there, is it worth it? I saw what it was like at the top. I not only lived it but saw the way others lived it too. Take this one guy, one of the most respected executives in this town to this very day. A lifetime in the casino business. He gave everything to it, blood, sweat and tears. He had four kids – the daughter had a child with a gangbanger, the eldest son has been in and out of jail on drugs charges, the goal for the next one was to be a Hell's Angel and the youngest died of an overdose. One day the mom got dressed up and blew her brains out. Where was the dad? All he ever did was work. Some high roller or executive came into town and he felt he had to pay attention to them instead of his family. The kids weren't bad people. They acted out to get attention. I know, because I was like that myself. I felt abandoned by my mother. I had to chase my dad around for weeks just to get him to sign a permission slip for me to play sports in high school. It just wasn't a priority for him, never mind taking me out in the backyard to show me how to swing a bat or shoot a basket.

I got out. One of the high rollers who was a client was making millions in the mortgage business and I went out to Orange County to work for him. I sat in a cubicle with a phone. It was a relief not to have to deal with people in your face, drunk, acting foolish, using anybody within grabbing distance. I made $42,000 my first month and for months after I was his top seller. But then the bottom fell out of that, as everybody knows. So I came back to Vegas again. It's familiar. It calls you. There's nowhere like it, as long as you don't get caught by something that pulls you down. You stay in luxury accommodation, see the shows, eat fabulous food. And the elegance of the properties is just astounding. If the Wynn/Encore isn't the best resort destination in the history of the world I'd like to see what is. Smiling doormen opening doors for you. It's a fantasy land.

I know a lot of people here. I can connect the dots for business people that need them connected. Also for visitors. I used to do it as a favour, but now I say, How much are you willing to pay? I look for partnerships of mutual advantage to increase my margins. For example, I work with nightclubs, selling the advertising space that in tougher times the billboard owners are having a difficult time selling. I get my fee in the services they provide instead of cash and then I package that with accommodation to sell at a discount to people who want to come to Vegas to have a good time. It's V.I.P. all the way. People feel important. I took some military personnel who had been in Afghanistan to a nightclub. They spent a few grand but said it was priceless. 'We were crawling around in the desert but now we're on the dance floor, drinking prime liquor, hot young women all around us. We're feeling really special.' To be able to make a profit from making people feel good is awesome.

Gaming is stagnant, but the clubs are booming. These places cost around $100 million to build now. They're set up with stadium seating, the little guys up at the back watching the high spenders at the V.I.P. tables down on the floor. It's like a sports arena. Steve Wynn said that the late-night shows are suffering because now people want to go to a club and *be* the show. What I've found is that when people go to a place they want to be around the most important person in the room. In a club the most important person in the room is the one who is spending the most. Business people know that too and over the past decade the clubs have really gained momentum in the business of setting up status. There are a lot of pretty young women working in these clubs. Basically a guy's got a two-hour window when the club is really buzzing to get attention. The more you spend the closer you get to the V.I.P. tables. Some guy who is working fourteen-hour days and is married with kids can come out here and suddenly seem interesting, be whoever he likes to be and see the effect it produces, as long as he pays. That's what separates Vegas from anywhere else in the world. You can live that fairy tale for a while. When you spend enough the waitresses come out with their little dresses waving flashlights and dancing around your table. It gets attention. It positively reinforces the image you're trying to convey. Doing two weeks of curls in a gym and rolling up your T-shirt might get you the attention you want in a small town in Indiana, but not in Vegas. You've got to spend. The dance-floor tables start at $5,000. I was at a club last night with a New York trader and a hedge fund manager and the bill came to $10,300. The trader paid and said it was worth it because he gets $1 million a year in business from the hedge fund manager and he wants him to feel good. A Saudi prince might come in and see that and think he's got to spend $20,000 just to keep face. Girls get $5,000 tips. I talked to one girl who made $40,000 in one night. It's a spectator sport. They've got Michael Buffer now, the announcer at boxing matches who says, 'LET'S GET READY TO RUMBLE!' He comes into the club and says that into a microphone after he's introduced the spenders. It's called 'bottle wars'. You can see it on YouTube. That golfer who was in the news bought a $90,000 bottle of champagne. There was one really titanic bottle war where a guy spent $200,000 in one night. The other guy got to one-fifty and said, 'I'm done.' The news gets around. It creates a mythology. 'That guy's a legend.' That's what they want to hear.

I'm in there watching this stuff all the time. This is the city of chips that look the same if they're worth one dollar or ten thousand. People lose any sense of the value of money. But I know that at the end of the day when the smoke clears I'm not going to have the resources to pay for that lifestyle. I'm not going to be one of the players everyone's looking at, a Derek Jeter with the flashlights waving and the girls dancing around. Or my dad, for that matter.

There are a lot of pretty girls in this town trying to figure out what to do with their lives. They land in from all over the world because there's money here. All they have to do is serve drinks and have fun. They hear the tales. Some guy dropped a girl five thousand bucks in chips, took her to Louis Vuitton. Everyone's a sales person, everyone's chasing the dream. It's the hope of hope, it's fantasy. Drop this token into the slot and become a millionaire in the next second. For a young attractive woman the goal very often is to latch on to the most important person in the room. He'll take care of you, almost like you're an employee. What's ten thousand bucks a month to him? Every once in a while he comes by for a visit. The dual-income template doesn't really hold here in Vegas. He's got money, she gets her hair and nails done. I've seen it myself. When my dad owned the Stratosphere I didn't have to talk to girls. They came to me. It was like I was Justin Timberlake. Then when the company stock went down, so did mine. That's the marketplace.

I had a girlfriend for four years and left her for someone else who turned out to be a drug addict. The pain of that break-up was immense. I'm off girls now, at least in terms of some loving, emotional attachment. If your girl is in the party scene and on drugs you're going to get hurt. And so is she. Her decisions are chemically affected. She wants to be around the most important person in order to feel self-worth, and now this important person she thinks she's found is between her and her regular guy. He's selling it to her that her life is going to change for ever, but he's probably going to grab her, use her and leave her. It's not like he's Prince Charming. There's so much confusion and pain. She takes more drugs then so she won't have to think about it. I've seen it all – this guy's a big deal, he's got six houses and his own plane. Then you find out he's a fraud on the run from the feds.

Basically, this is the same town it was in Benny Binion's day, or my dad's, in a lot of ways – a dirt town between Utah and California that survives by selling fantasy. There's a friend of mine, class valedictorian, field goal kicker, math wizard – perfectly suited in every way to a profitable business life. But he got into sports betting, made a million bucks a couple of times in a row, and now he's hooked. Life in a cubicle making thirty or forty grand doesn't look too interesting to him any more. I tell him, 'Take the paycheque, it's reliable. I've seen gambling money come and go all my life.' But he can't hear me. He's chasing the dream. I just heard about a guy who collected $2.7 million in insurance money when his wife died. He went to the casino, started out as a $10,000 player. The rumour went around. He started to get attention. The casino reps started to work on him – 'You can qualify for such-and-such a tournament if you bet this amount,' or 'We'll fly you to the All-Star game.' A few executives started hanging around, making him feel important. One day he won $400,000. Maybe that was the worst thing that could have happened to him. He started betting larger and larger, but now nothing panned out. In less than six months all the money was gone. He sold his car, lost his house. He just pawned his watch. He's got three kids, aged two, four and seven and he's living in some tiny little dump somewhere, dead broke. They got the job done

I've watched it every day, people who've put away money for thirty years dropping it all in one single night. What kind of state are they in? What kind of guilt do they carry, knowing they've just blown everything they could have passed on to their kids, that those kids are going to have to struggle through the public school system and fend for themselves? Sometimes they think, 'I'll pull myself out of this, I can hit that $28 million jackpot. I'll show 'em.' Or they get mad. When my dad got mad all hell broke loose. He was one of the meanest people I ever met when he got mad. I was the same. I knew how to cut because I was cut myself. I know that in the end he felt bad about a lot of things. Then what do you do? You medicate. There's plenty of doctors here who'll write the prescriptions. You try to keep your conscience quiet.

Nevada Stupak is founder and director of Stupak Las Vegas, a service providing customized accommodation, entertainment and food experiences in Las Vegas. While gambling remains stagnant, the club and pool party scene, says Nevada, is at 'an all-time high', and his business has expanded each year. He lives in Las Vegas, and is a vegan.

MACHINES

You see the banks of machines when you come out of your gate after landing at the airport. You can start playing as soon as you arrive, or in the last moments before boarding to leave. The facades of the Strip hotels all have a different theme, but each contains a large room you could fit an airplane in, with patterned carpet, waitresses ferrying drinks and hundreds of machines. They gurgle and flash, with images on them like those on children's toys. They are in corridors, bathrooms, restaurant terraces. Psychologists are consulted about optimal configurations of tight ones and loose ones. People slouch in front of them with ashtrays and super-sized drinks and hot dogs as if they're camped there, or watching their fifteenth hour of TV.

The casinos emanate out from the Strip and through the valley. There are small ones, such as those along Boulder Highway, and others like the Station chain which tower over everything else in their districts. Bars have machines along walls and video poker screens set into the bar's surface. Gas stations have machines. In the one nearest us there were four along a window opposite a rack of motor oil and another solitary one in the corridor between the gentlemen's and ladies' toilets. The car wash had one in the waiting room.

Just inside the entrance to our supermarket there was a tiny casino with dimmed lights and carpet and an attendant wearing a striped vest and string tie. People sat in chairs with their plastic bags of groceries at their feet, their faces lit up by the changing colours of the machines. A small woman with wispy, straw-coloured hair was often at the machine beside the door. I watched her over two years as her steps grew more hesitant and as she seemed to sink further into her frail frame. Sometimes she looked up, vacant, haunted. Her face seemed to be slowly receding into her skull. Maybe she was sick. Maybe she was trying to spend all she had before she died. But it was as if the machine was absorbing her life.

The machines tell you a different story each time you put a coin in. They can redeem you, cancel your debts, bring you to the promised land. You think, At least they should behave with some sense of mathematics, or justice. You are pulled in. You wait for it all to come good. 'Why is an activity with so little to offer so appealing to so many people?' asked a writer named Edward Allen, who used to drive in from Pahrump to the Vegas casinos. '[Why do we give] our money away week after week to people who do not love us?... Even if [the compulsive gambler] seems miserable most of the time, there is something very powerful about the instant the dice are thrown, the second the deciding card is turned over, the moment the little ball takes its last spastic bounce into the numbered slot...It is a neurological jolt made up of greed, lust and excitement mixed together with a strong dose of fear.'

Before I ever went to Las Vegas I heard a story about it from a friend of mine in London who had lived there for a while. He and his wife sometimes stopped and talked to an elderly couple who lived along the corridor from them, he said. They had worked for decades and saved their money and raised their children in the Midwest, and then when it was time to retire they sold their house and moved to Las Vegas. They were very happy there, they said. It was comfortable and safe and fun, and they loved the weather. One day my friend heard the old man shouting in the hall and went out. Men were taking all the furniture out of his apartment. The old man was trying to tell them they had the wrong place, he had no debts, they must bring his furniture back. The men kept working. Later the old man found out that since they had moved to Las Vegas his wife had put all the money they had saved into the machines. It was over a million dollars. They had to move to their daughter's basement in Iowa.

The machines never pause. They console you with their imagery, lure you with their caprices, light up and sing to you so you'll think you're winning even when you're losing. They're always there for you, any time of the day or night. 'The machine is my best friend,' said a man who'd lost his girlfriend and home to it. 'It's been in my life more than any person.' 'It was like a kiss from a lover,' said a woman of the machine that drove her to embezzle a quarter of a million dollars from her employer. 'It was sweet.'

You will see small signs here and there on the walls of casinos giving the local contact number for Gamblers Anonymous. The casinos will help put you in touch with them if you ask. The signs reminded me of an ad for Samaritan suicide counsellors I saw on the strut of a bridge high above the Severn Gorge in Bristol. They reminded me too of cautions on cigarette packs, for casino managers are trained to scent leaking blood. Anyone in a vortex of large loss will be given rooms, cars, alcohol, private jet rides and anything else that will keep them spinning. A barman once told me he watched a woman growing increasingly hysterical as she went through everything she had on a poker machine. She'd borrowed from friends, got all she could from her cards, had begged credit from the bar and was screaming that she'd kill herself. He tried to calm her down. He told her to stop playing, go home, get some sleep and when she was sober and clear in the morning she could think of what she was going to do. His manager pulled him over and told him he was never to do that again.

'We're not doing our jobs unless these people lose their cars and houses,' he said.

LOUIS HARPER

Student
Salesman

We drove all the way out here from a little town in Louisiana in 1989 with all our stuff in a U-Haul. There was me, my mom, my two older brothers and my sister. I was seven years old. We were coming in on Lake Mead Boulevard from the north. It was about one or two o'clock in the morning. And suddenly there it was, spread out over the valley below, this giant city, just glowing, sparkling. We were so far above it. Our town had, like, five thousand people. I'd never been in a plane before. I never saw a city from high up like that. It just took my breath away. It still does, more than twenty years later. I still drive up there on weekends. My mom pulled over to the side so we could have a good look at it. We all thought it was just gorgeous. We were mesmerized, without a doubt. 'We'll do good here,' she said. Or something like that. It was a long time ago.

My dad was a fireman at the local airport back in Louisiana and my mom stayed at home because he made enough money. She was a normal, stay-at-home mom, I guess. Meantime the economy out here was shooting through the roof. A lot of people were coming. It was like the Gold Rush. They'd heard the dealers were making four or five hundred dollars a night in tips. That's what my dad wanted to do, come out here and be a dealer.

He got here two months before us. He was supposed to go to dealers' school and find an apartment. Instead he got a job installing solar heating systems for swimming pools. It didn't pay very well and everyone working there apart from the owner was heavy into heroin or crack. You could see the needle marks on their arms. They'd come to work cranked up and then take breaks in the van and smoke pot. I don't know that well how my dad's drug use was before he came out here, back in Ohio where he was from or Louisiana. I'd say light. He had it pretty much together, I think. But by the time we got out here he was already into hard drugs and had two other women going.

Things went to hell in a hurry. My parents were divorced within a year. My dad gave up all pretence after a while. He left his drug paraphernalia right out there for you to see, a box with foil and a spoon and stuff like that on the table beside his bed. My mom got a cashier's job at Main Street Station. She met guy after guy. They'd move in for a while. Then leave. She's probably the laziest person I've ever met in my life. She got the idea that there were people out here with money she could latch on to. She was looking for the golden ticket. They all had money and drug problems. That was the template. She met a guy named Ron who was a slot mechanic and had been in the Marines. He's not the reason I went into the Marines myself, in case you might think that. I couldn't stand the guy. He was with us six or seven years. He had a military pension. A mortar had gone off in front of him in Vietnam. He had this huge scar.

My mom kept a padlock on her room and another lock on the pantry. She didn't want us getting to the food. There'd be some Kool-Aid in the refrigerator and maybe some leftovers. Sometimes she cooked macaroni and cheese. She worked in the day, went out at night. We had babysitters a lot until my brothers were old enough to do it. She smokes crack. Her teeth are blackened because of it. She says it's because her mother hit her once with a pan. When I was old enough I started to babysit my uncle's kids for twenty-five bucks a week. That took care of school lunch money

I'm the only one in my family to graduate high school normally. One brother went to jail as a freshman. Another eventually got his diploma in a federal penitentiary. My sister dropped out in her freshman year. My oldest brother got involved in a Mexican gang that'd steal cars and drive them around in the desert. Mostly Saturns. You just needed a pair of scissors to get into them. He was in jail four or five times before he was eighteen and a further three as an adult, most recently for domestic violence. He got into heavy drug use a long time ago and never came out. Three weeks ago he went over to see my mom. He went into the bathroom there and my sister walked in on him. He had all his heroin stuff in there, blood streaming down his arm and in his other hand a bag full of paint. He was shooting up and at the same time huffing fumes. That was the thing out here when you were a teenager. You'd go into a store and huff paint. Anyway, my mom gets this report from my sister and calls the police. She'd never think of taking him to a doctor or finding someone to help him. She'd have to know that sending him back to jail wasn't going to save him. She just didn't want to have to deal with him. 'Just get him out of my house,' she said to the cops. He's like her in some ways. He'll live with anyone who'll take him in. He lived with a prostitute, an actual streetwalker. The thing I got from talking with him is that because nobody really wants to date them they'll just latch on to anyone they think cares for them. She bought him a car and let him live rent free until he hit her.

We lived in a trailer, a double wide. We had a tiny room with a basket in the corner for dirty clothes. We cooked for ourselves if there was food and did our own laundry. Do I have a happy memory? I do, actually. I was hungry one day, there was no food in the house and my mom's door was open for a change. I went in and asked her for a couple of dollars for food and she actually gave it to me, just like that. Didn't bat an eye. That stands out. I stayed there in the trailer until I was fifteen and had a fight with my sister. I'd had a football injury that resulted in surgery on my knee and was at home with my feet up and a bandage on that circulated ice water. She said something that annoyed me, I said something back and then she threw a fan and hit the bad knee square on. It bent it right back. I went after her. I'd have hit her if I could've caught her, but I was too slow. She hacked at me with her nails and there was blood on my arm. There was a lot of shouting going on. My stepdad and mom came out of their room. 'I'm sick of this,' he said. 'It's either him or me.' 'Okay,' my mom said. 'I'll have him out of here tomorrow.' After that I went to live with my dad.

I tried to stay clear of it as much as I could. I had a friend called T.J. when I was a kid. His dad was a really nice guy. I'd go to their house and hang out, watch movies. I got away like that early on and kept doing it. I did all right at school. I was on the honour roll. I played football, did track and wrestling. I had the objective from pretty early on to be a military pilot. I got to number two in the R.O.T.C. programme in high school and was set up for a military scholarship to the University of Arizona until I got that knee injury and they dropped me. They thought I'd be ineligible for military service. A Marine recruiter told me I could sign a waiver about the knee and they'd take me. I went straight in after high school. I trained, then served in Japan and Iraq.

What happened to them all? Let's start with my dad. He just fell apart out here. People kept pushing drugs at him. His second wife was bipolar, extremely sweet one day and in a rage the next, throwing things at you. She was on drugs too. Finally he went back to Ohio to save himself. A friend of his from Louisiana gave him a jug of some kind of wine they'd brewed up in a radiator. It still had some anti-freeze in it and after he left it in the trunk of his car it seems it got worse and by the time he took a drink it had the power to just shut down his kidneys. Because there was no filtering effect it went straight to his brain. He lost his balance and eventually went into a coma that lasted a week and a half. My uncle was with him and called an ambulance. For a while they didn't know what it was, but eventually they figured it out and put him on dialysis. It looked like he was going to be all right. But then three weeks later, I guess he had a bad day or something, he took a beer, keeled right over and died.

My eldest brother is basically institutionalized. He's smart, probably the dumbest smart person I know. When he was in jail he scored high on an I.Q. test and they set him up for college, got him registered and everything. But he just took the cash and never went to classes.

My younger brother was going the same way, stealing cars, doing drugs, but that spell in jail early in high school saved him, in my opinion. What happened was he stole a car and drove over to my dad's. We felt that our dad could still relate to us in a way our mother was no longer able to. I guess my brother just wanted to be with him. Anyway, when my dad saw it was a stolen car he called the cops and my brother wound up doing time. He went to a place called Indian Springs Boys' Camp and when he came out of it he was fine, and still is, more or less. He never forgave my dad, though, for sending him down, never even went to his funeral. My dad had tried talking to him right from the beginning when he started getting in trouble and never got anywhere. He took a chance in calling in the law. He took the hit. Anyway, latest news on my brother is he lost a job at the Palms where he was making three to four hundred bucks a night and now he's a waiter at a topless place.

My sister is morbidly obese. She must weigh over three hundred pounds. She works at places like Wal-Mart sometimes and lives with my mom and a man who got some money from an insurance settlement after a motorcycle accident. My mom sent me a couple of birthday cards when I was in the service in Japan and tried to reach out to me when her sister got ill with cancer, but it was too late for me, really.

Can you blame a city for all this if you believe people have free will? I don't know. I know that everything fell apart in my family within three months of arriving here. I know that even if you're not familiar with this place, even if you don't know a single person, you can get hold of drugs in minutes. It's open all the time, inviting you to come in and wreck yourself. I never knew what 'last call' was until I went to South Carolina with the military. My dad's younger brother came out here. He used to do a little gambling in a small Mafia place in Ohio. His wife left him and he was working in the same pizza place he worked in as a kid. It wasn't a very good picture. His other brother, the one stable one, thought it would do him good to come out here and start over. He got a job as a craps dealer. He thought that gave him an advantage when he gambled himself, but of course this city is built on the house's advantage. He spends everything he has in casinos. He doesn't have a car or a phone. Gambling has torn him apart. The same brother who brought him here is now trying to get him out.

A lot of people who end up here are jerks. Not all, but many. They think, 'I'm a badass. I'm gonna take this place.' And they lose and lose. You only need a driver's licence to get a job valet parking. Ten or fifteen years ago it was a six-figure job. Same with working by the pool. That's no longer the case, but the mythology hangs around. You can set your life up pretty quick, but if you have an addiction, latent or otherwise, Las Vegas'll find it and you'll get eaten up. The casinos put up pictures of the big winners, but you don't hear about all the people they buried. This place is just saturated with depression. I was valet parking at the Wynn and I'd see them all the time. There wasn't a day went by when you wouldn't meet someone who'd dropped at least five figures. They'd swear at you, cry, then maybe go home and hit their wives, or whatever. You grow up here you see a lot of families falling apart. I saw too much of that too early. It kind of normalizes it.

I'm finishing up school here and working at CarMax. I sold a car to a guy yesterday. His card said he was an attaché at the U.S. embassy in Beirut. He'd have been combat-trained, earning a couple of hundred grand with everything paid, escorting politicians. He came into the lot with his suitcases and a gun case around his arm. He said he needed a car. I started doing my usual routine but he cut me off and said he wanted an Audi, with navigation, and he was in a hurry. He was tense, really wired up. He said he had to get on the road right away. I said, 'We can get everything done in two to three hours.' He said it had to be within forty-five minutes. He couldn't wait any longer than that. I showed him an Audi and he said, 'Okay.' He didn't test drive it. He didn't even look inside. We went into the office and he wrote out a cheque for $25,000. Before he went he told me he'd come into town the day before, checked into the Rio and went to the casino. He gambled right through the night and into the next day. He never even went up to his room. Early on he was up seven grand but in the end he lost ten. That's a common story. People come in sharp and make good judgements, but then all the free booze they give you starts kicking in. I could smell it coming out of his pores. 'If I don't get out of here,' he said, 'this city'll do me in. I won't sleep, I'll lose all my money. I'll crack.' Then he was gone.

After completing training in the Marines, **Louis Harper** was deployed to Okinawa and then completed two tours of duty in Iraq, where he served as a machine-gunner on helicopters. He was awarded combat air crew wings and two air medals. He had a plan to study for two years and then return to the Marines to qualify as a pilot, but a motorcycle accident disqualified him for service. When he was in my class at UNLV he told me he'd been diagnosed with PTSD as a result of handling dead bodies on what were called 'angel flights' in Iraq. Having blood all over his hands and arms and smelling the charred flesh of those killed in explosions left him plagued with nightmares. He graduated with a business degree and moved with his fiancée to Detroit, where he bought a house and is prospering doing mortgage brokerage work for Quicken Loans, a company he said is helping to bring about a renaissance in that city. His eldest brother died of a heroin overdose. His middle brother is married and still living in Las Vegas. He has no contact with his mother.

THE FOUNDER

Continuous life in Las Vegas began when William Andrews Clark bought a two-thousand-acre farm and water rights from a widow named Helen Stewart for $55,000. It was a bet on his own ability to sell it as a future boom town based on his plans for a railway spur that would pass through it on its way from Los Angeles to the Transcontinental Railroad further north.

It is worth looking at Clark for a moment, for some of the themes running through his life have persisted in his city. He'd driven mules, sold eggs and been a schoolteacher, but then became one of the three Copper Kings of Butte, Montana when he ventured into banking and was able to repossess the claims of defaulting miners. With a little of the money he'd made from the mines, he bribed his way into a U.S. Senate seat. In Las Vegas too he capitalized vertiginously on his investment, drawing three thousand speculators to his 1905 auction of parcelled-up bits of Helen Stewart's farm – a hundred times more than Las Vegas's then population – taking $265,000 in sales. He died aged eighty-six in his mansion on Fifth Avenue in New York, having survived his first wife and married a woman thirty-nine years younger who had been his ward as a teenager. When asked about having bribed the Montana state legislature, he said, 'I never bought a man who wasn't for sale.' He was an archetype of the Gilded Age, with a fortune among the top fifty accumulated in America. Mark Twain said of him, 'He is as rotten a human being as can be found anywhere under the flag.' The district in which Las Vegas sits is Clark County, named for him.

ALESHA BEAUCHAMP

Childcare worker

My dad's originally from Alaska and my mom from Florida. That could have been a family joke, if we had any. They met at high school in Boulder City, just outside Vegas. She was very Christian. They married when she was twenty and he was nineteen and planned what she thought was a perfect life – a nice house, steady work. He wanted two kids and she wanted four, so they compromised on three, all two years apart. First love for ever and church every Sunday…

But it didn't go that way. He was stingy and stockpiled money, she loved to spend. He drank a lot. He was rarely at home. I think he used to take on extra work just to stay away from her. In fact I have no memory of them ever being in the same room.

I was six when they divorced. I was the youngest. From that point on she was out all the time, either at work or with her friends. These were people who were into cocaine and gambling and drinking. There were dishes piled up in the sink for weeks. We'd throw apple cores behind the television. We were in a middle-class neighbourhood and ours was the house with the dirt front yard. We had to wear these hand-me-down clothes to school, which meant we were teased mercilessly through grammar school and junior high. It wasn't that there wasn't money coming in. She worked and my dad always sent child support payments. But there was never any food in the house. We'd go days eating peanut butter out of a jar with a spoon. She'd eat in casino restaurants. One day she came back with a bag of leftovers and we were hungry and asked her if we could have some. 'No,' she said. 'That's mine.'

How were the days? When I got up my mom'd already have gone to work. I'd get dressed, watch TV, go to school hungry. If she'd won I'd get lunch money, if she'd lost I wouldn't. Sometimes I'd get food from other kids. I'd come home, watch more TV, play with Barbies, go into La-La Land, as my sisters called it. I never did homework because no one ever asked me to. Whenever I'd see my mom she seemed to be furious. I don't know why. She screamed, threw things, kicked holes in the wall. Nobody ever wanted to come to our house, ever. There was no cable TV, no food, it was a mess and my mom was screaming the whole time.

There wasn't anything to make me realize this was abnormal, except sometimes when teachers asked if I was all right. They could see my clothes, that I was hungry, that I never did homework. They must have suspected that something was wrong at home. But I didn't get it. I was too young. It was just normal life to me.

There were a few unlikeable men. One was a meth addict. He came to live with us when I was ten. He was a freeloader, just vicious and rude. He worked for about a minute as a waiter but they fired him for stealing. He took my mother's charm bracelet and pawned it. It was a present from her father, something very precious to her. He knew that. He'd go out in the middle of the night and stay away for days, then come back and sleep. Eventually he was put away for writing bad cheques. Our family Sundays after that were spent going up to the jail to visit him. She kicked him out, but eventually took him back, at least for a while. In between he broke into our house and robbed us.

My sisters were in a constant war with my mother throughout their teenage years. They drank, smoked, did drugs in the house. They hung around with complete losers. Both of them had suicide attempts and abortions. My middle sister, Shawna, was the wildest. She was thrown out of school for carrying a switch-blade and went to prison for breaking and entering. When she was seventeen she moved into a meth lab in North Vegas run by a woman who lived there with her son. This woman swindled her in some sort of bank scam for $6,000 that my dad's still paying off. She went off to some other place in the ghetto. My older sister, Vanessa, got away to live with my dad and I wanted to go too, but my mom put all this guilt on me. 'You're going to abandon me, everybody's always abandoning me.'

I've worked with kids in recent years who have parents who don't pay attention to them. I can see why my sisters were as they were. Our dad was emotionally unavailable and our mom was falling apart. But at the time it just hurt. They wouldn't have anything to do with me except order me to change the TV channel for them. They'd beat me up. Their friends would come over and beat me up too. They were all cool because they were wild and bad and I was the nerd. I played soccer and did gymnastics and was in the school orchestra and choir. I loved that. I got pleasure from it, and some peace. My dad supported me in it, I think because he knew he'd lost control of my sisters. But when I came back home the pressure was on and I felt I had to hold everything in. There was some kind of unstated law that said I wasn't allowed to be angry, that I was supposed to be happy all the time because everyone else was falling apart. I used to bite myself. I'd see my mother screaming, breaking doors, kicking things. I didn't want to do that to anyone else, so I did it to myself.

My mom grew up dirt poor in a family with ten kids. I think she saw my dad, and the life she imagined with him, as the solution. When that didn't work she thought it would be us, then divorce and then clothes. She decided to spoil herself. Finally it was gambling. She'd go to crappy casinos on Boulder Highway and be zoned out for hours in front of poker machines. She poured all the money she got into those things. She wanted to escape and the 24/7 lifestyle suited that. When she had a boyfriend that's what they would do – sit in front of machines in casinos all night like zombies. The gambling seemed to tone her down. She wasn't so much angry as depressed. But through all of it – angry, depressed, whatever – she was preachy and religious, the uber-Christian. I think she always wanted to appear better put together than she was. But one time she went too far, and then she just couldn't fool herself any more. Shawna had got a job at Little Caesars when she was sixteen. My mom said, 'Just give me your cheques. I'll keep them safe for you so you won't spend them.' When Shawna asked her for some of the money – it might have been for a car or something – my mom had to tell her it was gone. She'd taken it for gambling. It was around $3,000. That tipped it for her, I think. She'd stolen from her own child. She could see how low she'd gone. She went to Gamblers Anonymous on her own initiative and hasn't done it since.

We all went after ruined men, ones who needed to be rescued and fixed, who look like they need a mommy. This city is full of them. My mom's now married to the brother of the meth addict who robbed our house. They got together just after he came out of jail after serving five years for drug possession. When I was in high school he took my viola and pawned it. When I told my dad about it my mom got mad at me. Vanessa, my oldest sister, is with a bellboy at the Bellagio. She broke up with somebody else then found him. She knew him from high school. She's an epileptic and pillpopper who swallows painkillers and valium like they're candy. They both do it. They spend money they don't have and are just about to lose their house. Shawna broke up with this guy she had three kids with and who used to beat her up. Now she's with a functioning alcoholic.

I did the same. I got together with a guy whose marriage broke up when he was twenty-four. He went to Costa Rica and made a failed suicide attempt. Then he went out with someone who cheated on him. I met him when he was in that wonderful state of mind and thought he was the one for me. I lived with him and his mom and stepdad, who used to brag about shooting black American soldiers when he was in combat in Korea. He said he shot his first black man when he was ten. He thought it was great. I thought, I'm living with a psychopath. My boyfriend was originally from Utah, prim, buttoned-up, Mormon Utah. He thought Vegas was the Devil's playground and he went for it

– poker, craps, but especially Megabucks. Obviously you're not going to win that. He was a waiter and he blew all his wages on the machines. It was his way of not thinking about things, like his ex-wife, for example. He wanted me to go with him and I didn't want to go and then when we got there he'd stay with the machines and ignore me while I'd drink myself retarded. People would hit on me and he wouldn't notice. He was emotionally closed and abusive. I could say, 'How do I look?' and he'd say, 'You could do better.' It could get much worse – 'You're fat, you're worthless, you're stupid, you're drunk.' His friends did it too. It was like home. Normal. I'd drink some more...Sadly that was the longest relationship I've ever had.

In those places you can drink for nothing. I'd black out. I've fallen down, been carried out of bathrooms. Nobody cares. The barmen just keep pouring the drinks. They'll laugh at you as they fill another one and you're heading to the floor. There's no cut-off, nobody saying 'last orders' like in other places. Some of them turn the other way when a guy puts roofie into a glass. My mom's had that, and my sisters. Girls get taken out semi-conscious from these spiked drinks and are raped in cars. I got into buying coke so I could drink more. I got taken advantage of. I felt awful almost all the time. I started cutting myself. I felt like I needed to be punished, like I was worthless and had to pay. It was a release, an adrenaline rush...It's hard to explain. Everything was such a mess, so out of control, and when I cut myself...it was like something was happening that was really supposed to happen. I remember sitting on a toilet drunk and high on cocaine and feeling so sick of myself and taking a straight razor and opening up my leg.

Being a young woman in this city sucks. All these images of strippers with manufactured bodies flash down at you from the signs. You're supposed to be the perfect Vegas party girl, the good luck charm perched up on a stool in a low-cut dress in a casino, a floozy who'll do whatever she's asked. You think that's the way you have to be if you want anyone to hang out with you. Be a bad girl, you're in Sin City. There wasn't a single time when I went to the Strip when I was in high school that a guy wouldn't scream something obscene from a car, or pull over and talk to me like I was a hooker. I've been groped. I was walking through a casino on my way to the restroom when a guy threw a drink on me. He made this kind of sizzle-sizzle noise and said, 'You're hot!' All his friends laughed. It ruined my dress. You become a shut-in.

I stopped everything when I was twenty-five. I started having panic attacks and got scared. I was ashamed of myself. I went to A.A. I went to seven different counsellors and then found one who really helped me. I stopped drinking and taking drugs, got rid of my boyfriend, changed my job. She listens, she cares. She made me realize I should care for myself more, that I'm not doomed to repeat my parents' mistakes. When I don't have much money she charges less. She's like a wonderful friend.

I work for a day-care facility in Henderson. I know how much these places can suck because I used to be put in them myself. I hated the people who worked there when I was a kid. I'd like to make it better. Kids have parents who are just decaying in front of them, who leave them alone night and day because they're in casinos, who think it's socially acceptable to be drunk at eleven o'clock in the morning. They can be left without food, like I was. They raise themselves. I never wanted to grow up because adult life looked so hateful. Now they have Kids' Zones in the casinos. They're like giant hamster cages where you can put your children while you gamble. That's the city.

You have to be very smart, very strong-willed to withstand it. There've been attempts to make it a real city with different kinds of industries, but when the economy goes sour they go back to what they know best – Sin City, come to us and be a whore or a man-slut and we'll look after you. It's always looking for your weaknesses. My mom worked with this woman for one of the unions here, oddly enough the one that represents the slot-machine mechanics. She was an addict. Slowly and steadily over a number of years she was operating this system where she was embezzling the union dues. It got up to $80,000 by the time she was caught. Of course she didn't have anything to pay it back with. All of this stuff that the city tries to hook you with keeps pressing in on your life. People just turn into the living dead. We don't educate them well enough to withstand what the Strip offers. The parents of my best friend at school, they were perfect victims for it. They started drinking and gambling in Laughlin when they were living just over the border in Arizona. Then they moved to Vegas and the drinking and gambling got worse. They got kicked out of their duplex and moved into a smaller apartment. They told my friend she had two days to pack from there because they'd lost that place too. They then moved into this place too tiny for her to fit so she moved in with my dad. They just kept going lower and lower. When she applied for a credit card she found out that her mom had already stolen her identity and got $4,000 in cash out in her name. She's still paying that off. She went to law school in Minnesota to get away from them, but they followed her. She can't get rid of them. They're such basket cases now that they can't look after themselves. Because of them she can't even imagine ever having kids herself.

It's hard to find normal people here. My dad says that. He was never with anybody after my mom and he divorced, until very recently. He likes to go to Red Rock Canyon. 'Where are the women who hike?' he'd ask. Sometimes I look on Facebook to see what's happened to the girls I went to high school with. Some became strippers right off the bat. I could see these postings from people going on about their all-night parties and their hangovers and losing their jobs. People here think they can go on being twenty-one for the rest of their lives. I don't do that any more. I don't want to live like that. I like to go to museums, theatres. You probably have to go away to see much of that, though. Every summer now I go up to the Burning Man Festival in northern Nevada. There are about thirty or forty thousand people camping out. It's self-expression and art. People walk around nude if they want to, they create things. At the end they burn this huge statue of a man made of wood. They're open, tolerant, nice to each other. It's a shock after Vegas. I'd got so used to assuming people were lying, hiding their addictions, checking you out to see how they can use you. Since I stopped living like that I don't have any friends.

I've got a boyfriend who lives in California. When I come back from visiting him and I'm driving in on 15 and can see the lights of the city out ahead of me in the valley I can think, That's home. That's where my bed is. I can get a nice memory, like playing with my dad at a water park when I was a kid. But when I get closer I shudder. Something cold runs through me. It's just such a terrifying waste.

Alesha Beauchamp and her California boyfriend broke up not long after this interview took place. She has held jobs at a welfare office and in telemarketing, but at the time of writing is unemployed and looking for work that will bring her into closer contact with nature. All her family still live in Las Vegas. Her oldest sister, Vanessa, lost her house, and is in the process of getting divorced. Her middle sister, Shawna, is married to a gun salesman. They have five children between them. Her father is married to a woman who shares his interest in hiking, and is prospering. Her mother works as a teacher's aide in a primary school, has not gambled for many years and remains married to the man who pawned Alesha's viola. He drinks heavily, has extreme mood swings and speaks of suicide. When Alesha was living in their home she was so uncertain of her status that she kept a cooler, tent and sleeping bag in her car. She finally got out of Las Vegas and is living in Oregon.

SIGNS

In Las Vegas there is a museum of discarded signs.

It is a city of signs. Times Square and Piccadilly Circus have been known for their signs, but these were signs that referred to products that could be bought all over the world. The signs of Las Vegas are about its own unique and central industry, or services dealing with its effects. Sometimes the signs refer to what they say you can get in the building immediately behind them. The MGM lion, the facade of New York New York and the Luxor beam that astronauts have seen in space are signs. Along the Strip are giant, moving-image screens showing fragments of Cirque du Soleil and magic and burlesque shows. The image changes just as the showgirl is about to turn towards you or her gown is on its way to the floor. The women on the signs tend to have a knowing, complicitous look. They might smile a little, wink. They seem to say, 'You and I both know what you want. Just take it.' There are signs that evoke the Old West, the boulevards of Paris or private clubs for discerning gentlemen, signs that announce bargain prices for roast beef or twenty-four-hour breakfasts at the casino buffets or the competitive pay-out rates at their slots. The gas station pumps have television screens on the top promoting casinos. You can hear them from the middle of the street. Signs are a significant sub-industry. They are to Las Vegas what tyre manufacturers are to Detroit.

Out in a semi-wasteland beside an airport runway to the south of the Strip is the vintage 1959 'Welcome to Las Vegas' sign that much of the world has seen. You could wait twenty minutes to get to the front of the line of people waiting to have their pictures taken under it. It's internally lit, with star, diamond and silver dollar motifs. It made it into the National Register of Historic Places. The world's largest bikini parade was held around it, presided over by the mayor. Its designer, Betty Willis, is likely better known to cultural historians and city residents than the architects of the Strip hotels.

The signs gather where movement is at its most dense and change in the nature of what they promote according to what kind of district they are in. When I drove in from Henderson to the university, I turned off the expressway at the airport exit. Here were Barry Manilow and Carlos Santana and Holly Madison, the Playboy model/stripper who had become a city icon. There were grinning comedians with sparkling teeth, Cirque du Soleil acrobats, ads for clubs with names like Bare, Rehab, Eve and Surrender, and one called Tao with a delicate Asian woman looking over her shoulder with hooded eyes, a long tattoo running up her naked back. A line of around a dozen bare-topped men in low-slung jeans advertised an Australian male stripper act called Thunder Down Under. There was a verité-style photograph of an uncertain-looking bellhop, his cap a little askew, kneeling on a hotel room floor beside some Roaring Twenties-style packing cases, caught by the camera with a blonde hotel guest, wealthy and predatory, wearing little under her fur coat, laying back and opening her legs in his direction. It advertised a Strip hotel with the slogan 'Just the right amount of wrong'. The signs around McCarran Airport tell you that in Las Vegas you can do what you can only dream about doing elsewhere, you can be bad, you will love it and no one will censure you.

Out on the expressways where the citizens circulate there are signs for teeth implants and breast enhancement and a lot of giant business card-style photographs of tough-looking lawyers in suits who understand how you accumulated such large debts, are angry about them on your behalf, and know how to conjure them away. They can also deal with your drunk-driving charge. Downtown, beyond the neon where the tattoo parlours and pawnshops and last stop before the street hotels are, the signs promote bail bondsmen.

If you drive north out of the city on 15, you pass the Nellis Air Force base and a speedway and the exit for the mythical-sounding Valley of Fire, climb over a small mountainous wedge of Arizona, then drop down into Utah, home of the Mormons. Here the signs are for bread, tractors, cough syrup. If there is a woman on them, her cheeks are the colour of apples and her blouse is buttoned to the neck.

CHRISTOPHER ERLE

Student

My dad juggled at the Excalibur my whole childhood. That's the Sleeping Beauty hotel on the Strip. He'd get up on a cylindrical tube and juggle three objects while balancing a flute on his nose, then throw the objects aside and start playing. Just before one of his more complicated or absurd tricks he'd say, 'I just want you all to know that I have a master's degree...which I'm not currently using.' I loved watching him perform. I was envious.

It's true that he had a master's degree. It was in musicology. He got it in Fayetteville, Arkansas, where I was born. His own father was radically unavailable emotionally. I only know him from what I heard and his Wikipedia page. He was a child prodigy who evidently learned to crawl and hold a violin bow at the same time. My great-grandmother was from Bristol in England, a quintessential pageant mom who marketed the little boy and had him playing the vaudeville circuit practically from infancy, executing sophisticated, technically complex music and doing it expressively. He married three times, became the concert master of a symphony orchestra in Japan and wound up teaching at Yale. His wonderful third wife, Syoko, still teaches the violin there. I studied Japanese partly to better converse with her.

My dad dropped out of high school. He sold flowers in a Boston subway and after his maternal uncle taught him the flute he played in an enlightenment cult that specialized in LSD-induced ecstatic states. Eventually he got it together academically and got his degree. And he married my mom. She was a marine biologist from Puerto Rico who later retrained as an occupational therapist. We all moved out to Salt Lake City, where my dad had been offered the musical directorship of the Utah Shakespeare Festival. Have you seen their reproduction of the Globe? It's pretty impressive. I saw Titus Andronicus there when I was three. Just the thing to guarantee you'll become a well-rounded person. I remember this girl with no hands and no tongue rolling around and moaning. I loved The Taming of the Shrew. In a lot of ways I've become Katherine, just as I've also become Sally Bowles.

The whole time my dad had this hobby of juggling. He was very ambitious about it. He can master something if he's interested. He's very smart. He used to open for the plays and somewhere along the line he was noticed by a scout or entertainment executive from Vegas and they offered him the gig at the Excalibur. In a single bound we went from high art to the depths of kitsch. Vegas is a very tempting place to work. It draws from everywhere and has the greatest concentration of talent on the planet. Plus Vegas paid him way more.

We lived in different places, usually around whatever school I was attending. I've had my fair share of meth-addicted, alcoholic, Jerry Springer Show candidates as neighbours, loud and boisterous and inarticulate in their anger. We all have here. There were also stable adults. I can't comment much on the meaning of that because this is the only place I grew up and I don't know the national ratios of stable adults to crackheads. I just got on with my own life. I always had something going on. From the age of five or six it was obvious to anyone that I had a strong desire to perform. I saw my dad do exciting things and I wanted to be exciting. I played the piano early – Bach, Telemann, Scarlatti, mostly Baroque stuff. I got into being a gymnast in grammar school. I felt very defined by that at the time. I could do hand springs, front and back tucks, little tumbling sequences. I was very hard on myself and so embarrassed if I failed that I'd have to leave the room. I progressed quickly. My parents were very excited by me when I was little and doing these things, but I think for them as my childhood faded so did some of my magic…but maybe not. I'm not sure.

My dad always read to me. They gave me advanced books from a young age, like Bullfinch's Mythology. I was a Hellenist before I knew what it was. I loved going to Caesars Palace to see the talking statues in their robes. Dionysius was very real to me. He was a hero. I had some kind of subliminal instinct for liminality and dichotomies – like with Apollo and Dionysius. Comic books have mythologies that comprise these things. In the nineties they were culturally relevant and innovative. I developed a huge affection for the characters, like Aeon Flux. I was very drawn to the way they struck erotic poses.

It was a Mrs Harris who taught me to read. She was a wonderful, sweet woman. She had a day care centre in her home that I went to. I don't think about that house much if I can help it because her son molested me there when I was five. It wasn't just me, it was every kid who went there. She didn't know anything about it until she came home one day and saw the cop cars out front and us being interviewed.

I was bored with gymnastics by the time I finished eighth grade. It wasn't quite performance, at least of the kind I was starting to aspire to. I started to pick things up from these amazing people who came to our house – magicians and sword swallowers and fire eaters. They'd bring their toys over and do tricks. I asked them how it worked and they showed me. I learned to do certain bullwhip tricks with targets that I was later able to apply as a prostitute. Above all, I wanted to be an acrobat. I tried juggling, but I didn't have a passion for it. It didn't have this immediate, otherworldly grace that I saw when I watched an acrobat.

I was a fearful, introverted child. I was afraid of roller coasters, cars, animals. Performance was my way of coping with it, of taking risks on my terms. I knew myself and my own body while I had no control over cars and animals. I added new techniques when I was a teenager. Middle school is just a mean, amazingly savage place. Kids at that age have a sense of social hierarchy but no wit or wisdom. There was a short kid named Mikey who used to torture me in P.E. I'd like to see him now so I could rip open his jugular. My strategy then was to pretend I was crazy. I talked to myself and when I talked with others I did it in the voice of a gutter punk. I put unnerving things on my binder. Mikey thought I wanted to kill him.

This was an act, but in fact I wasn't so well. I had chronically bad dreams that would make me very nervous. I was visited by little impressionistic memories of being held down when I was five by Mrs Harris's eldest son. I became loud, vulgar, confrontational. I smoked openly, talked back, sold pot to other students. I realized at fifteen that the movie stories of cowboys and princesses were complete and utter lies. I lived in this seedy city, this cornucopia of bad decisions and raunchy tastes and foul language and failure and I wanted to be seedy myself. I looked for people who were darker, a little less pure, tainted somehow, certainly less cute. I hated cuteness. I kind of took on this debaucherous city's foibles and ailments and both lived them and eventually performed them. To not do so would amount to putting myself in quarantine in my own city.

I went to high school at the Las Vegas Academy of International Studies and Performing Arts. There were a lot of pills flying around. People wanted to live the Iggy Pop lifestyle. I always knew I was gay and started to come out. It was a performance school, it was pretty gay anyway. I embraced punk rock in tiny venues and hung out with older kids who were squatters or had heroin addictions or had been to jail. I was always with older people. Even as a toddler I gravitated towards my dad's friends. My boyfriends too have tended to keep pace with my parents' age. All in all my behaviour was troublesome and outrageous enough for me to require therapy and to be kicked out of school.

Something changed. I can't quite put my finger on it. I just know I lost my fear. Something inside me woke up. I graduated high school by testing out of all the requirements and started college at sixteen. A professor published an autobiographical essay I wrote in a textbook called The Red Rock Reader. Performance took a new direction. Once when I went to see my dad perform there was a Mongolian contortionist named Otgo Waller on the stage before him. She was in a duo contortion act where they folded their bodies in half and did one-arm handstand tricks and balanced on each other. I was spellbound. It was just sensational and beautiful and magical to me. They were birdlike. They were also like statues as they turned so magnificently slowly on one arm. Here was that liminality again. There was something post-human about it.

I trained myself in contortion and eventually Otgo became my teacher. My parents supported me in this. I got my first gig at a county fair in Arizona – very exciting, two grand for two weeks. I hung out with very debaucherous magicians twice my age and had my own brief cocaine phase. I enjoyed being the kid. Later I got a gig with Andrew S. and Kelvikta the Blade of the Swing Shift Side Show. They were wild. They swallowed swords and passed all kinds of sharp metal objects through themselves. There was a lot of body modification around them. I met someone who'd implanted horns into his forehead. Both Andrew and Kelvikta had bifurcated tongues. He had an act where he screwed a thick metal coil into one nostril, which then travelled all around his face until it came out of his mouth. It wasn't quite enough from his point of view so he started doing it with an electric drill. Kelvikta's specialty was Pussy Darts, where she put a blow gun into her vagina and shot darts out of it. The first time I ever saw her was at a birthday party where she blew out the candles of a cake that way. It was magical. I rolled around in glass and drove large nails up my nostrils and folded myself into a little Plexiglass box. We did a special event in Albuquerque for fetishists and goth-industrial kids. Andrew had the World's Largest Genital Piercing and put two fists through his scrotum. Kelvikta did her Pussy Darts and Sleaze the Clown did a fire transfer from torch to torch with the end of his penis. The crowd went nuts. They couldn't even imagine being that happy. Eventually the owner gave us some cash and told us to run for it because the cops were coming.

I loved the flux, where your body is a project, a constantly morphing entity. I put six to eight gauge hooks through my back and was suspended by them over the stage. In the show Freaks we did at O'Shea's on the Strip we pierced live. You can still see the scars. One day after a show my back hurt and I asked my mom to look at it. She said I'd damaged quite a lot of the connective tissue but that it would grow back. It felt like jelly. I had to leave a literature class once because blood was leaking through my bandages.

I hit a real low point when I broke up with a professor of mine at college. My tendency has been to date career-obsessed, emotionally unavailable men. Maybe I think I'm going to be them when I grow up. I was so in love, it was the first time, and when he left me I became violently depressed. I wound up in Los Angeles with a glass of milk, a bunch of pills and a plastic bag to suffocate myself with. I pulled myself out of that, but I was still shaky. I was looked after by my parents for a while. I wrote furiously about all the things that happened to me in so short a time. It was a slow process. I'd had a huge mental breakdown. I got a little stronger then and got a very dull job writing business plans. Something like that just couldn't work on its own. I missed feeling interesting, to have adventures and something to say every day, like when we were chased out of Albuquerque or I was flying over the stage on hooks. I felt the need to be on stage somewhere crude. I'd worked for a while in a tranny hooker bar over in Commercial Centre on Sahara serving cocktails. A waiter I slept with got me the job. He told me I'd have to wear almost nothing. 'Even better,' I said. That was a time when there was a lot going on. The cast of Freaks used to come in. The staff loved them, especially Little Miss Firefly, the World's Tiniest Female Performer. People used to slap my ass and grab my balls. I took it a step further and started stripping – one of those staple entertainment industry jobs here in Vegas. I was an immediate hit. I had a shaved head, a strip of coloured hair and this jaded look. I did contortion tricks and had this acrobat/slut/erudite personality. I was way more raunchy than the Ken doll dancers around me. I'd rub my crotch like Madonna in the nineties. There was a champagne room for private lap dances. I could dance all over them or else just sit spread-eagled on the couch, touching myself and talking about Fauvist colour theory. There was a certain strain of customer who really got a kick out of that. They felt special because they thought I was special.

One night a man at the club asked me to come to his hotel room and strip for him. I said no, but one of the regulars had heard this and said, 'Come with me,' and doubled the price. I just decided to do it. I went back to this palace he lived in and fucked him. He wanted me the next day and I did it again for a large sum of money. I played waltzes and mazurkas for him naked while he kissed my neck. I started doing it regularly then. It became my gig. I'd go to a bar, look for someone ordering top-shelf liquor, someone who wanted to be seen to be spending. I'd get into a conversation. Even as far back as high school I was alert to the subliminal, non-verbal waves in an encounter. I would tune in, invade a person psychologically, make up a kind of dossier on them with multiple scenarios and then steer them in some direction. If I could see them becoming interested in me and that they were about to make a proposition I'd mention some radio programme or newspaper article about sex workers I'd say I'd read, just to see how they'd react. Then there would be some process until we would, or wouldn't, arrive at a business arrangement.

I certainly never felt myself to be a victim. In Vegas prostitution is not slavery, it's a vocational decision. The predator/victim scenario is the other way around. We're in their heads and they're never in ours – that is, if you're any good. You seem sentimental, but never are. You seem close and affected and in love, or whatever they want, but you never are. Of course you do meet a fair complement of utterly intolerable, narcissistic and neurotic men with unlimited petulance who are arrogant about their wealth. I was with one for two days in Los Angeles who started screaming at me in a club because I talked casually with a few other people while he was doing the same. He threw my phone across the hotel room later and spent the night pouting, and in the morning it was me who apologized. That's somewhere in the fine print of the job description.

Las Vegas is very Futurist, in the ways it embodies speed and dynamism and technology and the violence inherent in the city's own break-neck evolution. We build things we know we will get rid of. They're like stage sets. Nothing lasts – jobs, buildings, relationships, families. Everything has a fly's lifespan. Flies live and die so quickly they don't even realize they are themselves. Vegas taught me a lot about the importance and limitations of speed. It taught me about self-awareness, mostly by observing people who don't have any. This is the city where it's okay to be vain, it's okay to have nothing to say, to be unoriginal and derivative, a complete victim of somebody else's marketing ploy of what you should be and how you should behave. It's okay to be a drone, and you might be really successful at it. It's the city of quick fixes. You get disillusioned with one franchise, just re-illusion yourself into another. You learn to be interesting. I learned. Of course everything is insubstantial. You get a gimmick. 'I'm not the computer itself, I'm just a cool feature.' You are utterly the sum of your parts. I was a fun little trick – he's young and vulgar, but educated and musical and also into sado-masochism and swallows swords, etc. Vegas taught me that performance is not just something that happens on stage. Performance happens every minute. It is every interaction you ever have with anybody, it's the awareness that somebody else is the audience to what you project. You can't survive here and look for substance or be sensitive. It's not allowed. You become detached. I want to be the camera, like Isherwood. It's living in this environment so long that made it easier for me to be a prostitute.

Half of me is what it is because of Vegas, and the other half despite Vegas. I've become de-sensitized because of Vegas, angry, competitive, dissatisfied and rough around the edges because of Vegas. But I've also become honest and curious despite Vegas. I've observed and seen what I had to transcend.

This is not a curious city. It wouldn't work. It's predicated on anaesthesia. It requires a compliant, innocuous, non-resisting populace. Just look at what arrives by the planeload every day, almost every one of them with a sense of entitlement because of what the city says it is. An asshole comes to Vegas and thinks he has the right to act like an asshole. Some of them might even think it's a duty. To be a woman in Vegas is kind of like being Penelope when she's on her own and defenceless and dealing with all the aggressive, predatory, entitlement-minded suitors. The city will find these people's neuroses, their insecurities, whatever they're susceptible to, and get them to spend money to advance those insecurities and in doing so to advance Vegas. And all the rest of us that make up the populace here spend all our time serving them. The most surprising thing about me in Vegas is not that I swung on hooks or stripped or became a prostitute, but rather that I like to talk about James Joyce and Virginia Woolf, that I like to sit down and write or to compose waltzes that juxtapose nineteenth-century melodies with post-Schoenberg forms reminiscent of Bella Bartok. That's the shocker. This isn't a city about people or ideas, it's about how the room is. I've seen attempts here to create a counter-culture, some kind of reaction to the mainstream media and the ideas entangled with them. Whenever something authentic begins to grow the city comes in and puts its brand on it. I've seen attempts to create an arts scene, like our First Fridays downtown in our tiny, anaemic arts district with homeless people as far as the eye can see. People go because the galleries offer free Sangria. I've seen bands come and go. I've been in a few myself. Realistically if you want to be in a band you'll be playing covers of Journey songs in a casino lounge. I once had an offer to be in a Bruce Springsteen cover band, but I said, 'No, sir, I'm too good for that. I'm going to keep stripping.'

I got caught in a variety of the proffered vices here, but never gambling. I got cured of that early, when I was sixteen. I had a gig at a Volvo convention at the Venetian. I was walking through the casino pushing a cart with the little box I folded myself into and my hand-balancing canes and I stopped dead in my tracks. I saw this woman at a slot machine smoking a cigarette, occasionally sipping at a cocktail while she fed in her coins, completely magnetized. Now that's not normally a sight that would make you pause for thought in a casino, but the fact that she was in her wedding dress…I mean, Happy honeymoon, doll. That just sold me on the idea that I'd never gamble. It wasn't the guy who lost his house, it was the bitch in the wedding dress.

What do I think will happen? I think that Vegas will survive, and there will be something inherently sad in this. It will stubbornly persist in what it is. It will steadily become an old woman, withered and broken and severely weathered, who just can't seem to die, like my grandmother. Everything about it will lose function except for the actual presence of life. Vegas is a zombie and it will keep going because zombies don't die.

I like a lot of what Vegas has done to me. I don't wish I had a simpler life. I don't wish I came from a middle-class family in the Midwest, thriving on ideas I'd got from the Disney Channel. I enjoy being a bookish version of Courtney Love. I've aged prematurely, but I'm happy with that.

Christopher Erle was twenty-three and a student in his final year at UNLV by the time all the things he recounts here had happened. He graduated with an exemplary record. Shortly afterwards he was raped at gunpoint in his own home by an assailant high on crystal meth. Later that year a man with whom he was involved was shot dead in a Las Vegas bar by an ex-boyfriend. It took him, he says, around a year to recover from these events. Early in 2013 he moved to Atlanta, Georgia to begin a new life. He got a job in advertising, sang Serge Gainsbourg songs in a bar in the evenings and began writing a novel. He was very pleased to no longer be living in Las Vegas. But in the summer of 2014, traumatized, perhaps, by the loss of his job, he jumped from a balcony in an attempt to kill himself. He is back in Las Vegas being looked after by his parents, who hope he will recover from the brain damage which has impaired both his memory and his speech. His progress, so far, has been good. He is reading, reacquainting himself with his past, writing and hoping to go into a PhD programme in English literature.

BOMBS, WEDDINGS, VICE AND THE DESERT

The little city boomed for twenty years after William Clark's auction, then staggered. A rail strike provoked the removal of the maintenance works up to Caliente in Utah and then everyone could see how fragile it was. The desert was right there on the edge, waiting to take it back, as it had Petra. It had nothing to sell. It would have to dance and sparkle and allure to go on living.

It tried resorts, even grassless golf, but vice was easier. Its hinterland was a vast terrain of parched earth and drifting men who worked the mines and railroads. It offered them prize fights when no other state in the Union would. Block 16 was an openly operating brothel district. Gambling and Prohibition laws were noted, then unenforced. When a Senate investigation in the 1950s leaned on organized crime, mobsters from all over America migrated to Las Vegas, where they knew they would be left alone. They skimmed millions in untaxed casino profits and settled deals with poison and ice picks. They were the City Fathers, looked upon not only with esteem but with a kind of tenderness.

Marriage and divorce became absorbed in the general deregulation. Nevada set the lowest residency requirements for either, then kept trimming them. You can drive in and get married as you would drive in for a hamburger. You can be serenaded by an Elvis impersonator. You can have a vampire minister at the Goretorium.

The father of a student of mine had been a wedding chapel minister for twenty years. 'Did he attend a seminary?' I asked. 'It was just that it didn't work out when he tried selling insurance,' he replied. One minister reported, 'I've been doing weddings ten years and I have done a little more than thirty-seven thousand. Eighty-six is the most I've done in a day. I did one wedding on stage in a total nude joint. I did a commitment ceremony one night for a man and his motorcycle. I had a lady came in one day, had a couple of attendants with her were all dressed up. She wanted to marry herself.'

Las Vegas shuns control, but the government saved it several times when it was failing, first with the Hoover Dam, then with two military bases during the Second World War. They tried to keep the dam workers in dry, chaste and non-gambling Boulder City, but the workers got to Block 16 and the gambling halls nevertheless. After the war the testing site for the Manhattan Project was moved there. New entertainment features came into being, such as the Miss Atomic Bomb contest, the Nuclear Hairdo and the Mushroom Cloud Party. 'It was a wonderful place for what the customers wanted,' a waitress at the Desert Inn's Sky Room said in the early fifties. 'They would sit around and listen to our piano player and look out the big windows and see the pretty hotel fountain and the guests swimming in the pool and the traffic speeding by on Highway 91, and then, just when they were getting tired, the A-bomb.'

Las Vegas has boomed and busted more starkly than most cities I know. Reading its history is like watching the bellows of an accordion as it plays a slow air. The city is optimistic, as gamblers are when they roll the dice, but also insecure. The desert intensifies this. It is everywhere. Its dry, split surfaces are like harbingers at roadsides and between developments. Lawns and pools and air-conditioning and mall walkways where you are sprayed with chilled water cannot entirely make you forget it. You feel its scale and silence at night. You know it can disorient and starve and kill and it's right there and that in the history of Nevada there are more ghost towns than surviving ones.

MELINDA MEDINA

Mother

I remember it was snowing, I was a little girl, and I remember going into the house to hug my grandpa and my mom pulling me out of there. She put me in the car and tried to get away but the wheels were spinning in the snow. She was crying. My grandpa came out and he tried to put chains on the car but my mom wouldn't stop. She just kept pushing down on the gas and spinning the wheels and crying. My uncle came out and he pushed the car and we got free of the snow and out onto the road to Vegas.

That was in White Pine, by Ely. I loved being there. My grandpa was a very loving man. He worked in the mines. I'd get up with him at 4.30 and hang out with him until he went to work. He and my grandma wanted to keep me but my mom wouldn't let them. They fought. She was…she was very pretty and a lot of the guys wanted to take her out on dates and she was young and she wanted to go. She got pregnant with my brother and my grandparents raised him like he was their own. When I was born they wanted to do the same with me but my mom wouldn't let them. She said she got tricked once but it wasn't going to happen again and she took me down here with her to Vegas.

I heard a lot of stories about who my dad was. I never could get to the final truth. Somebody said he was called Fabian, somebody else said George. I also heard Frank. It's not like there weren't people who knew. They knew but wouldn't tell me. My uncle and his wife, for instance, but they kept their mouths shut. My mom always looked tense whenever I asked her about it. The only thing she said was that it was the same man who was the father to my brother and she couldn't tell me any more. My grandpa said he met him and I believe him. He was a married man and he felt he couldn't acknowledge us because of that. My grandpa said to me, 'He don't want you, baby, he don't want you. Don't pursue it because it'll break your heart.' I'm native Blackfoot, Cherokee and Tiwa, and maybe a little Spanish. Somebody said that my dad was Tiwa too, but he's Tongan. I know that. I remember the drums, these Hawaiian kind of things.

My mom was dyin' to get out of Ely since she was thirteen. She always told me, 'Don't ever go back there. That place is hell.' She liked money, fancy clothes and cars. She had a picture of all that in her head and I guess it was our bad luck she chose Vegas to go after it because, even though it's all around here and you can get it, it makes a mess of you usually. She was a camera girl, a cigarette girl, a cocktail waitress. She did all the casino jobs. I didn't see her much. There was a guy called Bob, an entertainer. She dated entertainers all her life. He was a bass player and Elvis impersonator. He built houses too and he'd put her into whatever spare one he had. She cheated on him, he cheated on her, and then there was Steve. He had money and took her skiing. I hate to say this, but she...dated...whoever. She was real beautiful, guys would take her out, buy her gifts, get her condos. She dated realtors, lawyers, an F.B.I. agent who tried to play dad with me. I remember all their names. She'd meet them in casinos. There was Chuck. He was married and he set her up in a townhouse. She'd go off on trips or live with them a while, just leave, no call, nothin'. I'd get left with friends of hers. I was just five, six, seven years old. It could be months. My grandpa'd come down on my birthday or something. He loved me. He'd bring me pine nuts, he'd store snow for me. But my mom leaving me like that, that scarred me.

My mom and I were both scarred. My grandma used to hit her when she was little. I had this perverted uncle who molested his eldest daughter for years and tried to rape my mom and later tried to get his hands on me. I remember him touching me. My grandma always defended him. 'That's my baby,' she'd say. I just heard from my cousin Brett that his sister Brenda blew her brains out because of that. And the other really big thing that hurt my mom was that she lost my brother. She never got over that. That was just one of the things she didn't get over.

The one she was with the longest was Richard, a Mexican. He was with us from when I was ten until I was nineteen. Richard's in jail now where he belongs. He had nice suits. He was a pit boss for the Binions. Ted Binion was the only one in Vegas who'd hire him after all his felonies and that was because Richard helped him get his drugs. He went to all the Vegas parties and he was drunk all the time. There wasn't a family gathering where he wouldn't pull his pants down and say, 'Kiss my ass.' He stored his cocaine in my room. My mom beat me when she found it because she thought it was mine. She threw it all away. When he came home and found out he didn't care any more and just started screaming at her, 'Do you know how much money you just flushed down the toilet?'

My mom had two kids with him. He was out drinkin' and druggin' and she started getting sick. She had cancer four times over. There was only me to look after those kids. I still feel like they're my own. Pamela, my little sister, she's grown up now. She's had a boob job and works in a club where she wears just the tiniest clothes, but she's going to college and wants to work with cancer patients because of our mom. I'm proud of her for that.

I was kind of naïve about boys. My mom taught me to cook and clean and do a lot of good things, but even though she'd always been with men she didn't know how to talk to me about them. When it came to that she just stayed quiet, except that I wasn't allowed to have boyfriends. She was real strict about that. But she loved Spanish music and she let me go to these Mexican dances they used to have at the Union Plaza downtown, and that's how I got raped and kidnapped when I was sixteen and just disappeared from the world for six months. I was with friends and we were driving somebody home. We had the idea we'd drop her off and go back to the dance. In the back seat there was this Mexican gangster type of person and all of a sudden I felt a gun in my back. 'Say you like me,' he said to me. He got me into a shed and raped me right there and then drove me to Littlerock, California. I was put in a blindfold and kept in a cement room on his parents' land. They were part of some programme that had to do with veterans who had gone crazy and they put them in those rooms. His parents didn't even know I was there for a long time. He said he'd kill me if I said anything. Eventually he told me I was to say I was his girlfriend and he moved me into a room in the house and I used to sit around the table with them all and play that role. His name was Rudy. He's dead now. I heard he got stabbed. When I was there with him I used to look after his son. I got kind of attached to that little boy I was there so long. I used to think about him later. I tried to get away twice but didn't make it. I found out later my mom thought I'd run away because I used to do that then. Rudy always used protection. That's one thing I'm grateful for. He had a brother, Angel, and Angel said to him that what he was doing was wrong and when their mom heard them talking about it that was it. She told him he had to let me go. He said to me on Mother's Day, 'I'm only letting you go because of my love for my mother.' He drove me back and she came with us all the way to make sure he did it.

Later on at school I had a boyfriend. His name was David. If he ever tried to get physically close to me I'd feel very uneasy. Rudy called to remind me he'd kill me if I told. I used to have these dreams that he was chasing me through K-Mart. I dreamed about my uncle, too. I'd see his fat shadow at the end of a hall, I'd feel his hands on me and wake up just as I was about to scratch his face. I told David and he said to come home to live with him. His dad was in the military and his mom was Korean. I felt safe with them. I had these little jobs, like maid jobs. That was the first time I tried crystal meth. A friend said, 'Let's try this,' and I did it. It made me feel better. I got pregnant with my daughter Alicia and I stopped using right away. But David was using too and he kept going. I couldn't accept that. I moved back to my mom for a while, then with a friend of mine called Tracy, and that's when I met Michael, who I thought was just awesome. He moved fast, he wanted to live with me right away, and I wasn't sure, but then I got pregnant with my second daughter. My mom told me to forget about both of the dads and just come and live with her. I think she wanted my children because she'd lost my brother. But I stayed with Michael. We was doin' fine for a while. He was working at Planet Hollywood and I was going to computer school. We had more kids, four altogether. My little sister, Pamela, was living with us too. It was good, or at least I thought so, but then I found out he was using cocaine and on top of that he was unfaithful to me. He'd even tried it on with Pamela. I came home and found her cowering in a corner.

I had such a lot of pain in me from day one, but after I left Michael it seemed my whole world just started fallin' away and I could do nothin' to stop it. We were having custody battles and he was stalking me when I was out with the kids, just staring, saying nothin'. I met a guy at my church I liked a lot – the whole time I was goin' to church. Michael saw me with him and I guess he didn't want any other man around his kids, he couldn't stand that, so he just kidnapped 'em. They were gone for eight months. I reported it at the Henderson police station. I was looking for 'em. I found out later he'd been moving them around places like Salvation Army shelters. While that was goin' on my mom started getting sicker and sicker. I was lookin' after her. I watched her dyin' in front of my eyes. She was so beautiful to me then, she said she was sorry for everything and she was proud of me and loved me. She said everything she had to say, and I'm so glad even now she did it, but whenever I asked about my dad she'd say, 'I don't feel well now. Can we leave it?' She never said. I know she was in love with him.

She'd told him a long time before how she'd die alone out of love for him and now she was doin' it. When she went I couldn't even get her pictures and things because the Salvation Army came and took it all away before I had the chance. I was back in that heartache, just dyin' inside because I didn't know where my kids were and after losin' my mom over and over through my life now it was for good.

I started goin' down. I was drinkin', usin' meth again. I couldn't pay the utility bills. I lost my house. I felt so alone. I felt like I'd been alone all my life and now I had all this time to think about it. My brother'd come to my mom's funeral. I could see he was doin' well and I was happy for him, but I could also see that safe life I could have had but never did. I was livin' hard, with friends sometimes, or in shelters. I lived in hotel rooms and paid for it by selling blood. My kids showed up, but I was too far gone. They put them in foster care. I was a bus stop drinker, or if I got twenty bucks I'd spin it out for two days in a casino playing penny slots and drinkin'. One time I got caught fallin' asleep.

I heard about the tunnels under the city. I had friends who were from there. I met Manny from drinkin' with him in the streets. I knew he lived down there. He was always good to me. He protected me, he never came on to me. I felt safe with him. He was a ticket hopper, from Alaska originally. He'd go around the casinos checking for money left behind in the machines. You might find hundreds of dollars that way because the people playing are often drunk and they forget. He said I could come down there and live with him. I was scared, it was so dark down there and unknown. But he promised me no one would hurt me. His place was off Flamingo there by the railroad tracks, under the Rio. I made him walk in front of me. We had miners' lamps on our heads. When I got there I could see it was like a normal room that somebody would live in, with shelves and a little bathroom with a curtain and a king-sized bed, all nice and neat. I freaked out the first time I slept there. I thought, What's happening to my life? But it was safe, just like he said. We had a sofa, a radio. We swept it out every day. There was always somebody with me down there. People would go to the wealthy neighbourhoods lookin' for stuff they'd thrown out and then bring it back and pass it around. They all had different personalities. One guy had porno all over his wall, another couple, Catherine and Steve, they had, like a house, with a kitchen and barbecue and everything else a house would have. There were fights sometimes and one girl, she used to freak out on speed and she was a klepto. You had to watch out for the rain and get all your things up high for when the water came flooding through. People lost everything that way and even got killed. Sometimes days would go by without me leavin'. You'd have to wear shades then when you went out 'cause you were so used to the dark. I got to feel like I didn't have to be in the outside world, and then when I did go out I couldn't wait to get back to the tunnel where I could hide. It did the same thing for me as drugs. When I was down there I felt like I didn't have to worry about anything.

Things got kind of rough. We lost everything in a flood and moved over to the Mandalay Bay tunnel. Then there was a fire in there. One day Rich Prenksa of Help of Southern Nevada came down and said, 'If I were to offer you your own apartment right now – lease, keys and all – would you take it?' It was my daughter's birthday. I thought about it, I wasn't too sure, but I said, 'Yes.'

Manny and me have our own little place now. I've been clean a year and a half. We're tryin'. I saw Manny help a blind man across the street the other day. I wasn't used to seein' that! (Laughs.) Actually there's a bunch of us from the tunnels living in the same development and we all look out for each other. I've got a case worker who cares about me. He calls me his 'project' and I call him 'dad'. We joke around. I get therapy. I've got a lot of pain and I know I've got to fix myself before I can do anything else. This is the city where it all happened and I'd get out of it if I could. But my kids are here. I see my oldest daughter every weekend because she's seventeen now and can do what she wants, but the others are still in foster care. I haven't seen them in four years. They won't let me see 'em until they decide I'm ready for that. So I'm waitin'.

When I look at Vegas I just see pure devastation. My mom got caught up in it and her husband too. I hate to see all the shows on TV that glamorize it, all that money and shopping and selfishness. My mom wanted it before she ever came here and it just made her want it more and more once she got here. Everything is right there for you, all the time. You don't think how much you're gonna have to pay for it later. I could get whatever drugs I wanted just by smiling at a guy. I went to Chicago once. It felt so good. It snowed on Christmas morning. It was so beautiful. I'd live there if I could. But I've got to get my kids back. I stay awake and think about them. My mind goes around and around.

Melinda Medina no longer lives with Manny or in the home they moved into after coming out of the tunnels. She has been reunited with her children and is still in Las Vegas.

HOMES

We pulled into the desert when the Mazda began to weaken through the hills and heat not far from the Valley of Fire. There was just scrub for as far as we could see. We took a walk while we waited for the engine to cool. There was a shallow bowl in the desert floor and when we walked down into it we saw cans, a plastic sheet, a burnt-out fire and a twisted shirt like the limb of an olive tree.

We saw encampments like that beneath bridges, in parking lots, alleys, empty spaces between buildings. In North Las Vegas there is what is called the Corridor of Hope where people live in tents on the pavement. Out on the road we saw tent cities outside Fresno and Sacramento. We saw improvised shacks and tiny trailers baking in the sun in the Mojave Desert all on their own beyond power lines and water supplies. There was a whole village of them near the Salton Sea. You feel you are looking at the traces of a migrating tribe.

There are reported to be around fourteen thousand homeless people in Las Vegas. In one primary school, eighty-five per cent of the children were judged to be homeless or on the edge of being so. Rich Prenksa, who went down into the storm drains and offered Melinda Medina an apartment, said, 'I don't believe there's a tree or a field in Las Vegas that doesn't have someone living under it.'

In frontier times the Chinese built a doppelganger city in tunnels beneath the streets of Livingstone, Montana to house their opium dens. Las Vegas has its own version in the three hundred or so miles of storm drains in the valley. A combination of warm weather, desert meth labs, psychological wounds among veterans, family tragedies, alcohol and gambling addictions has created a shifting population of around two hundred to a thousand people who have made their homes in the tunnels. They are, Rick Prenksa has said, probably the most successful at being homeless of those who are homeless in Las Vegas. They identify their addresses by the casino they live under.

KAITLIN REAVES

Student

We owe so much money all around. It's just terrifying to think about it. There are the banks, the credit-card companies. There's a long list of unpaid taxes. Each month there are payday loans at ridiculous interest rates and unpaid utility bills. My dad used to call my sister or me to hide the mail so my mom wouldn't find out how bad it was. That happened almost every day. Water, gas, electricity and phone have all been turned off. Both sets of grandparents have been bailing us out for years, so there's all that money that's owed to them. There was a second mortgage on the house and with all that going on I wondered how long we'd be able to keep it, until just recently when my dad did a short sale. We're renting now.

It started small. They came up to Vegas from Kingman, Arizona. My mom had jobs there, but she didn't get one for a while in Vegas. Maybe that made her depressed. Maybe she felt useless. I don't really know because I was a baby. I just know that she started drinking. My dad used to go to this little bar around the corner to get away from her. He'd say he was just going for a couple of beers, for a break. Like all those places in Vegas they had these video poker machines built into the bar and he started playing them. He won a few thousand dollars at first, then he started losing. He'd just lie then, he'd say he was going for groceries or to pay some bill and he'd be gone for six hours. I didn't understand. I felt lonely.

I think they feed off each other. The one is the other's enabler. Sometimes she made me go to the bar and get him and then if he came back she'd yell at him or be nice to him to get him to give up, but eventually she'd just get drunk. That really bothered him at first, but I think, now, that it's an escape for him. He can do what he wants, he has an excuse. She drinks beer and wine, but sometimes hard liquor. We got into a fight once when she was drunk on Captain Morgan and ordered my boyfriend out of the house. Once she was drinking Bacardi Citron and smelled like Lemon Pledge for days. She quit work and said to my dad, 'Why should I work when you just take all my money?' She's kind of a full-time drunk now. We make her go to the garage because she chain smokes. She has a camping chair in there and a TV. She doesn't eat. She's tiny, her eyes are sunken in. Her hair is short and dishevelled and she wears my dad's T-shirts. There are wine stains around her mouth. She drank five litres of wine once over a weekend. She has a nurse friend who had to come over with an IV to rehydrate her. She looks psychotic. She more or less lives in the garage and I think she likes it because she doesn't have to see anybody.

The money just goes, evaporates, like it's been sucked into some hole in the sky or earth. My dad's paycheques go on debts and what he gambles and then he gets these payday loans. It's constantly a desperate situation. He's pawned his guitar, sold our car. He's taken money from my sister. He's had my graduation money, my savings, my student loans. Once I phoned him to check my account and when he had my log-in details he transferred money from my account to his. He's taken money from my pockets. I still had $60 after being on vacation with a friend's family and when I looked later it was gone. That was him. He used my social security number to get a credit card when I was in Reno one time and ran up a thousand dollars on that. I work full-time and go to school. I have to pay all that off. I love him very much, he's a wonderful man, but it's…frustrating.

One of the stranger things about them is that even as they trash themselves like that they still seem to worry about what the neighbours think. I keep a hookah in my room and they tell me I should keep the blinds closed.

The last time I remember us being happy as a family was when we went to Disneyland. I was seven. I remember my dad driving, him doing up my hair in our hotel room. I had these white overalls. We had ice cream. I think I didn't know for a while how bad things were. My sister was older than me and she protected me when I was little. She was almost like my mom then. But I lost her too. As soon as she became a teenager she seemed to be around the worst people she could find in the city. She got terrible grades, she was angry and wild and defiant. She was already taking cocaine in eighth grade, I think. She drank, took speed, mushrooms. She loved to go to the

Strip and party. She got into fights. She had various boyfriends who sold drugs. One of them was particularly terrifying. She even had friends whose parents were dealers and who gave their own kids drugs. She could go into these rages. There was this one time when I was in sixth grade and my dad came in and she demanded to know where he'd been. He said, 'Nowhere,' and that just set her off, she started screaming at him that he was a liar, that he'd been gambling, that's all he ever did. She was punching him, hitting him. I got in the middle to stop them, which was stupid because I'm so tiny, and she pushed me so hard I went over the dishwasher. Then she kicked me. My mom tried to stop it too but she was drunk and fell over. I had a bloody nose and a black eye. There was so much screaming that the neighbours called the cops. She sulked for days.

She's a lot calmer now. She has a nice stable boyfriend who really looks after her. We're friends. She told me she was sorry for all that happened in those times.

My parents didn't have time to pay attention to us. They were too absorbed in their addictions. I used to have to get my mom up when she worked and she'd still be drunk. When I went to my first high school dance she was in bed. She didn't help me get ready, check how I looked. We ate cereal a lot. I was a cheerleader in high school and in the student council and gave speeches. They never came to see anything. With my mom, it's like she's just not there at all. She could be very aggressive, violent, like my sister. I could get into a physical fight with her and it was easier to hit her because I thought, That's not my mom, that's some crazy woman.

I had my own time of defiance. I could go out and come back at three or four in the morning. My dad could be on his way to work. They didn't even ask where I was. You get the feeling it's not relevant to them. A lot of parents here are like that. They ask their kids for money, they stay out all night. There were various times when a bunch of us would be at someone's house and be fifteen years old and smashed at three in the morning and the parents would come in and just say, 'Hey, catch you later,' and go to bed.

I know they feel bad. My mom cries. She talks about killing herself when she's drunk. One time I was sitting at the computer and I looked up and saw her reflection in the mirror holding a butcher's knife to her wrist. She didn't do it. I don't know if she ever would, but you live with the thought of it. As for my dad, I've talked with him about it many times. I've begged him to go to Gamblers Anonymous. I've told him I'll go with him. We were sitting in the car once and I felt so desperate about it and I was pleading with him, 'Don't you care about us? Why don't you stop? Can't you see that you're killing us? Don't you love us?' He'd always say, 'I'm sorry.' I'd see tears in his eyes. It just seems to own him. But I can't not love him. I'm very close to him. We do Star Wars marathons, we read and talk about books, we play golf. When I was little he used to play the guitar and I'd dance with my teddy bear and repeat words like 'toothbrush' or 'banana' over and over in a nonsensical song that went along with the tune he was playing. He thought it was hilarious and I did too. When I got older he taught me to play. 'Little Sister' by Elvis was an early favourite of mine. He's really funny. We could go to the supermarket together and he'd run up and down the aisles acting like he's mentally challenged, talking with a lisp. He's a total dork, just like I am.

It makes me feel bad to live in a city based on something that takes so much from people. They look so sad, so lonely when they gamble. I wonder why they do it. When I drive I try to look at the mountains rather than the Strip. I've yet to meet anyone brought up here that hasn't been pulled under by it in some way. It's just this minimum-wage place where everything bad for you is available 24/7, where everything is about what you can get right now and where no one connects. If you're not getting groped at a bar you don't have a social life. Men just come up to you and grind on you and think it's all right. In high school people already start to show some of the same symptoms as their parents, just falling into the traps Vegas sets. A lot of girls I know became strippers. One of them got a boob job as a graduation present to herself with money she got from stripping. It's like they don't feel they're worth anything unless they're naked and being looked at. If you don't have that certain look the city asks of you, if you don't have money or you're not in the nightclub scene, you feel secluded, like you're on the outside looking in at something. It's all so sad, so wasteful. It's obvious that these things people put so much time and money and belief into are not going to last, but they just go blindly on. They don't want to think about what will happen when it ends or when there's some kind of reckoning. It would be too bleak. You just kind of live with that here. It becomes some sort of normality, but a normality that's full of tension. For a long time I had bad anxiety problems. My sister once put me in a cooler and sat on it. The feeling of living here is like that, of being trapped, overwhelmed. I'd have these night terrors where I'd sweat and lose my breath. I used to smoke weed to deal with it, but now I meditate.

I know I'm going to have to get out if I'm going to have any kind of life. It's a 'no tomorrow' place. Everything about it is telling you that. When I was in high school the science teacher used to play 'Dead Puppies' in class. He'd talk about the weather, the news. I think he was on drugs. When I was out for two and a half weeks after a tonsil operation I asked him what I'd missed. 'Nothing,' he said. There's no real concern for education or the environment or art or any of the things that sustain you. I graduated, I think, fifth in my high school class. I had a 4.3 average. But it didn't make me look forward to adult life. It's hard to grow up here, or even want to, when your parents are falling apart. You know you have to grow up fast, but you don't know what to grow up into. Your parents are supposed to be anchors, but they're the ones that need guiding. I felt like I had to be the parent. The adult world just looked vile. Greedy, but also hopeless. I watched them, weak, passive, just accepting everything and endlessly repeating the same mistakes.

Kaitlin Reaves graduated from UNLV with a degree in English Literature in 2012. She worked as a substitute teacher while writing poems and attending spoken-word events in downtown Las Vegas, then entered a master's programme in counselling. Her father finally attended Gamblers Anonymous and no longer gambles. The debts he accrued are steadily being paid off. He and Kaitlin usually spend Sunday mornings together, playing the guitar and talking. Her mother veers between depression and drinking and remission from these things. Her sister is a hairdresser, lives in Reno and in 2015 gave birth to her first child. When she finishes her degree, Kaitlin hopes to move to Colorado.

BACKSTAGE

It took a while to get a car. We passed on a couple that were pulled out of warehouses in back streets by men who smelled of cologne and bourbon. We saw a lot of men like that, in pool halls, drugstores, bars. They tended to be thin, well groomed and to look like roués, with nervous tics and reptilian glares. We were about to buy a car from a Mexican cleaner, but she crashed it on her way to deliver it to us. The pale gold Mazda was sitting in a parking lot out at Nellis Air Force base. We bought it from a career soldier who'd been born in the Philippines. The tyres were parched and split like the desert floor and there was a complicated system involving a rope that snaked into the back seat for opening the trunk, but it ran with a tractor-like endurance, like he said it would. We put over thirty thousand miles on it by the time we left, and it was still able to do more.

Las Vegas can be very hard on you without a car. The distances are vast, the heat in the summer makes you feel you are inside a smelting works and it could take half a day to get some places by bus. But with a car we could look around. We drove one evening to the Strip and went north along it at a creeping pace through booming music and past the amusement palaces that rose around us in giant, brash cartoonish images and colours like some kind of electronic flame. If you are not actually dazzled by it I think you cannot fail to be impressed by the enormity of capital and effort they are willing to expend in order to try to dazzle you. Later I got to know a little the great writer and ponderer of beauty Dave Hickey, who made the same drive with his wife when they first got to Las Vegas. He wrote, 'It's all about the lights. Their profligate brilliance, I think, goes a long way towards explaining everything, because these lights, these millions of gratuitous lights, don't light government buildings, or monuments, or corporate headquarters, or famous heroes, or saints, or steeples. These lights sizzle and dazzle and smoke, and light you up. They are there for you. They invest you with grace and embrace you with their shadowless illuminations. So right in the middle of this wild desert town, surrounded by the black oblivion of hard, high desert, surrounded by the gloomy, sleeping ambience of dark America spreading away, there you are, in the middle of everything, glowing like a Renaissance saint.'

As we made our way up we thought we should walk around a little. We didn't know then that you could park for free in casino garages. I'd bought a round of drinks for three people in a Henderson piano bar and it had cost eighty bucks. We thought that maybe everything was like that – show tickets, mojitos, parking, scrambled eggs. So after we passed the entrance to Caesars we turned into a side street. We found a pot-holed, private but unguarded lot and decided to take a chance on leaving the car there. It was so dark after the blaze of the Strip that we had to wait a moment before we could see. We stepped out. Two goths huddled by a wall looked up, then back to something one was holding in her hand. In the lot were two tour buses, a camper van and some cars with large men sleeping in the front seats. There were discarded clothes, cans, a burnt-out fire, some escort magazines. We were in the nether regions behind the Flamingo. Out on the Strip was a dramatic, uplit facade; back here were overflowing bins, concrete walls that seemed to seep black grease and an exhausted-looking cook smoking a cigarette under a single light bulb in a cage. The door behind him opened onto white light blasting down on the Flamingo's entrails. It was like stepping backstage between acts — on one side blooming trees and the balustrade of a castle, on the other pine struts stretching the canvas flat and a stage hand sipping from a flask.

The city doesn't particularly want you to see the levers and pulleys behind the scenes, but it doesn't go to great lengths to hide them either. Everybody, after all, knows that Las Vegas is a stage and everybody's moving too fast to care. So you will see a lot of backstage sights there, even if you are just visiting. You see them in the encampments under the freeway bridges, the last look at a ring at the entrance to a pawnshop, the sudden eruptions of rage by strangers, the faraway look in the eyes and the grey-yellow pallor of the faces at the slots, the smashed cars with the drivers beside them blowing into a police bag. We were once waiting for a lift in a Strip hotel parking lot. It was around 2 a.m. and we were going home. The doors opened and a man of around sixty with dyed hair and dark rings under his eyes stepped out in a kind of trance and headed for the casino floor. Under a long cashmere coat he was wearing pyjamas and slippers. The stories told in this book are backstage stories.

So much of the theatrical can leave you with a yearning for the real. The real is suddenly and starkly there right at the city's edge and extends for thousands of square miles of desert and mountain and canyon with which human beings can do almost nothing profitable other than to leave it be and just look at it. Rattlesnakes slither, Joshua trees supplicate. Rocks endure the aeons of their life spans. It is vivid and dramatic and beautiful and has the sparseness and pitilessness of those areas of confrontation with the self that are recorded in holy texts. Right next to the contemporary world's own Sodom and Gomorrah.

It invites you to drive out into it and we often did, Las Vegas trailing off behind us like a radio losing its signal. We saw peach trees and springtime in California, buffaloes in the snow, the pink siltstone organ pipes of Bryce Canyon. Once in the Navajo lands in Arizona we stopped at the ruins of the seven-hundred-year-old village of Betatakin, set into the alcove of a red sandstone cliff. It looked as delicate as lace from the vantage point high above it. Not far away was the Black Mesa coal mine. Many villages like Betatakin, some say up to a thousand, were destroyed by the dragline buckets that created the mine. Thousands of Navajo were driven from their homes. The water table went down and became poisoned by chemicals. Sheep died and the subsistence agriculture on which the Navajo depended became impossible in the region of the mine. It wasn't easy for the mining company to get the rights. For the Navajo coal is the liver of the world. Cutting into the skin of the earth to get it is a kind of evisceration. A Mormon lawyer put together his own version of a tribal council when the others weren't looking and got the signatures he needed. Senators and national officials did their part for the mining company. Navajos have been fighting the deal since.

We drove north from there through quiet land. Outside of Page by the shores of Lake Powell there rises the gigantic Navajo (sic) Generating Station, a coal-fired plant that pours out 250 tons of sulphurous emissions night and day, polluting to the equivalent of 3.5 million cars. The coal leaves the Black Mesa mine by chute and travels by rail up to the generating station, where it is converted into the power that pumps water to Phoenix and ignites the lights of Las Vegas that shine for you.

GIOVANNA SARDELLI

Theatre director

I t was still kind of a small city when I was growing up, less than a million people. A big military gathering or a rodeo or a business convention of some kind could totally change the flavour. I grew up in a nice secure neighbourhood, largely Mormon. It's such a peculiar city, with the tension between licentiousness and religion. We make our money from what are vices elsewhere, but also have the greatest concentration of churches in the nation. In some parts of Vegas, the Mormon families would stand out, because the dad had a respectable job, there were eight kids and the mom stayed at home. You might have a lawyer, a barman and a magician, all in the same Vegas middle-class neighbourhood. You could see your friend's mom going to work in almost no clothes. But ours was mainly Mormon when I was growing up. My dad used to water the lawn in a Speedo and at first the Mormon parents used to tell their kids not to play with us. We were the only ethnic family there, us and Herb Mills from the Mills Brothers.

My dad opened for the Mills Brothers. He used to tell jokes and twirl guns. It was amazing how he picked up things like that. He and Sammy Davis Jr were supposed to be the fastest gun twirlers in the West. He's a full-blooded Italian who was born in Brazil. He came here as an illegal immigrant. He headed for Detroit to work in the car industry. One time he was in Kansas City and got into a fight in a bar and – it must have been one of those magical moments – the bartender threatened dire conse- quences and then said, 'You can either fight or you can sing.' So he sang, and then just kept on doing it. He sang at supper clubs and Italian festivals all over the country. He met my mom, who was a ballroom dancer. If you were an entertainer in the 1960s you went to Vegas. He worked on the Strip, singing Spanish songs, Italian classics like 'Volare', some Sinatra. He'd do country songs in his Italian-Brazilian accent. We'd sit in the audience when we were small and he'd sing right to us.

I watched his shows all the time. We travelled with him, around America, to Puerto Rico. When I was ten we went to Thailand. I thought he had the best job in the world. He worked an hour and a half at night and got standing ovations. People adored him and he made a good living and still we had all this time with him. I could see the power he had, but also how much he loved it. I knew from when I was a little girl that I wanted to do something like that.

I think I fared better than a lot of kids in Vegas because my mom was really a mother. She raised us. She was at home and she was both stable and attentive. She was also very active in the community. She got involved in creating legislation for retarded children and worked for Opportunity Village, which is a disabilities charity here. My dad helped with benefits. They were sociable, they had show-business friends like Robert Goulet and Pat Boone and Vic Damone and they had these big pool parties and spaghetti parties, but the destructive aspects of Vegas didn't appeal to them. They didn't drink or gamble or take drugs. My dad worked on the Strip, but he hated the Strip. We'd go to his shows and then he'd come home with us. He saw the debauchery and waste and was repelled. He could also have fun with it, though. Sometimes he'd try to scandalize the tourists. When we were waiting for the car to be brought up he'd scold us for being on the craps tables again. We were just little but we'd rub our hands and say, 'But them bones were *hot!*'

I was kind of nerdy in high school. I was just unpopular enough not to feel the pressure some people did. And I didn't see the city in the same way as a lot of the other kids. From the time I was in high school I knew I was going to leave and that I was going to be involved in theatre. It came from all the travelling I did with my dad, especially to New York. All the things I was learning to love – museums, theatre, ballet – weren't offered by Vegas. I always danced – I was mediocre at it, but I did it. But plays were the main thing for me. I was in plays from junior high on. I also got into Seido karate. I was looking for something that was social and athletic and spiritual all at once. That it was goal-oriented also suited me. I'm a second-degree black belt. But the thing that moved me forward, that got me out of Vegas and into the world I wanted to be in, was that I was a good student. I went to UNLV to study theatre, then to NYU for graduate school. Once I got to New York, I stayed.

I put myself through school by being a cigarette girl. The mom of a friend of mine had the cigarette concession at the Tropicana. I also sold flowers. People just threw money at you then. The artist who was doing the murals at the Tropicana called me over to his table and said, 'Why are you selling flowers?' I told him I wanted to go to NYU. He bought every flower I had on my tray and said, 'Now go home and study.' Just that. He didn't have any motive. He used to do that every month. That was my idea of work then – you show up, somebody gives you a few hundred dollars and you go home. People think it's still like that, but I don't think it is. I might have been in the last generation that didn't have to strip. I knew people who did it. You certainly could do well out of it. It seemed for some strange reason that every female studying psychology at UNLV was stripping. But you could still do really well out of the other jobs. We had these little cigarette-girl costumes, but you were reasonably well covered. There was some decorum. Now everybody seems to dress like they're hookers.

Men are being continuously over-stimulated by sex here. They come here believing that all women in Vegas are essentially available for them, that you'll eventually get what you want from them if you pay enough. You never see the best of men here. It's a city full of men with tan lines where their wedding rings normally are. The marketing of the city gives a man license to be his worst self. I was walking here the other day and a man said, 'You're pretty but you're old.' I thought, Well, I didn't ask. You learn growing up here that everything is marketed, everything is money, every sexual act and every state of mind has a price tag. It's a dirty and nasty town, but it has an honesty to it.

I thought when I got to New York that money moved an awful lot of things there too, but people didn't admit it. Here it's clear, it's right in front of you. If you've got your eyes open you can see that if you don't define yourself clearly, you're doomed. One time when I was selling cigarettes I got called over to a table. They bought some cigarettes and gave me a $2 tip. Then the guy said, 'It's my father's birthday. Would you kiss him for fifty bucks?' I said I wouldn't. It went to a hundred, eventually five hundred. It was just a kiss on the cheek, it was a family thing in a public place – I'd have done it if they'd just asked me and not mentioned money. I just couldn't sell it. My parents – how they lived, what they said – made the layout of the city very clear to me. I knew I had to be sexy in order to sell cigarettes or flowers in a casino, but that didn't mean I was for sale. I was just the sales device.

Sex is confusing for anyone growing up, but here it's weighed and valued. Even as a young girl you're leered at, sized up. Little girls become aware of their power very early. I think my older sister was seduced by that, while I was repulsed by it. It was the seventies, and she was experimenting. She got pulled into the seedier side of Vegas. She tried different kinds of drugs, battled different addictions. She didn't want to stay at home a minute longer than she had to. On her eighteenth birthday she had a piece of cake, said good-bye, got into her car and was gone. She went to Idaho for a bit, but came back because the money here was easy. And the easiest money was from stripping. I don't know. She couldn't have had a better example from home than she did. There were times when we weren't sure if she'd make it. I went to UNLV instead of somewhere outside of Vegas because of her. We were just waiting, hoping there wouldn't be bad news. She was really incredibly talented, a brilliant actress. I got into NYU because she guided me through my audition piece. My professors wouldn't have known how to do that. But there was no outlet for her here. She got her fix...dancing, basically.

She kept going in that as long as she could. She always stayed in touch with me. She wrote me letters. Eventually she became a cab driver. She fell in love with a man, he was another cab driver, and she really seemed to be getting her life back together. Then he had a heart attack and died. I really think she'd have ended up healthy if that hadn't happened. But it was really hard for her to recover from that. She died in her sleep, of an aneurism. She didn't OD, but you'd have to say that the way she'd lived had taken its toll.

More than a child of Vegas, I'd say I was a child of the desert. The desert came right up and into the city, all around. You'd see it breaking out in the vacant spaces among the houses and then stretching out as far as you could see. If I just stepped outside I was in it. It was this great wilderness playground for us. We'd play this game, 'Let's Find Al Bramlet'. He was a Vegas union boss who'd been murdered and whose body hadn't been found. Kind of sick, I guess. We'd build forts, climb on things. And it stayed like that for me. When I was a cigarette girl I'd see people taking their money out from underneath a pile of bills they hadn't paid and cash it in for chips. I'd see little kids left in a corner while their parents gambled and they'd still be there hours later. The desert became a kind of antidote for me to the debauchery and misery. It's quiet, it's slow. I can sit on a rock for hours. Maybe I got it from my mom, who was into Transcendental Meditation before anyone else I ever heard of. When you're in the desert you have that silence, that ascetic quality, and you have a sense of the animals in it and what they do. You have that image of the snake shedding its skin. I still come out here twice a year from New York to sit in the desert and do that, to shed skin, to let go of whatever has to be let go. Or watching the hawk soar. The desert really helped me. You have to be very clear here. It's so easy to get pulled under. Having a goal, a dream, that couldn't be met by Vegas gave me strength. Maybe if I was a better singer and dancer I'd have stayed. (Laughs.) Maybe I'd have had a career more like my dad's. But I got out.

After leaving NYU, **Giovanna Sardelli** was a stage and television actress for ten years. She then returned to study at the same university's Directors' Lab and has been a theatre director ever since, developing a national reputation for work on new plays. Since the interview her mother died of Obstructive Pulmonary Disease. Her father lives alone in the family house, where in the aftermath of his wife's death he was visited by veteran Las Vegas comedians Marty Allen, Pat Cooper and Shecky Green, who were determined to make him laugh every day. Giovanna and her sister, Petra, wrote a play together called Basking in the Neon, about growing up in Las Vegas.

WATER AND TIME

When we first got the car we took it out one morning and kept going for two hundred and fifty miles, to Flagstaff, Arizona. We had lunch, then came back home for dinner. It was late August and we wanted to feel cooler air, see a different kind of land.

Don't do that, said our landlady. Just go to Red Rock, or Lake Mead. You'll get snow up on Mount Charleston if you wait a while. They're right outside of town.

Lake Mead sparkled a pretty Pacific turquoise in the haze. The land heaved up in ripples and mounds of brown and beige and orange-pink, then striations of white where the water level had fallen. The lake, made out of the Colorado River by the Hoover Dam, is, at full capacity, the largest reservoir in America. But drought had reduced the run-off from the Rockies that made the river surge. Some marinas had closed. People said that the marinas had to keep picking themselves up and running after the disappearing water.

In the city, land in its native state is cracked, and as desiccated as ash. At night, on our balcony, we felt the air cool and dampen as the sprinklers came on and poured water over the fairways and cart paths. The sprinklers had automatic settings and flowed even when it rained. Our development had three pools and a Jacuzzi and was covered in grass. The city's humidity, we heard, could be up to eight points higher than in the desert next to it.

You can learn something about Las Vegas if you think about

water and time. It is in the nature of both to be measured. If you place water and time in relation to one another and to city in the desert, there will be something inexorable in the way they interact. Such as, if the city in the desert uses too much water, the time will come when the water will no longer be there.

George Bernard Shaw once said that a nation should be no more conscious of itself than a man is of his bones. I'd never met any place as conscious of itself as Las Vegas. It conceptualizes and brands itself incessantly. The form this takes depends on the exigencies of the era and the imaginations of those doing the conceiving, but most of the time the city is telling you that the odds can be beaten – you at the Megabucks slot, it with the waiting desert. It does not place itself syllogistically into the inter-relation of water, time and city in the desert. It does not think of water, or time, in the way they are thought of elsewhere. It behaves not as a city in the desert, but rather as one in the tropics.

Its two springs made the grasslands that surprised a group of Mexican traders into calling it Las Vegas, or 'The Meadows', when they came upon it in 1829. Paiute Indians had been drawing water there for centuries. The Great Basin Aquifer that came down from the north and fed the springs was so abundant that when rain fell the underground water shot up in geysers. People alive today once swam in Las Vegas groundwater pools. But the city pumped out so much of it that the land out around Nellis Air Force base began to collapse in on the vacated underground caverns. Afterwards there was the seemingly infinite supply from Lake Mead, but by the time we got there it was down to thirty-nine per cent capacity. A paper published in 2008 gave it just a fifty-fifty chance of surviving beyond 2021. There is still underground water nearby, but large amounts of it were radiated beyond use by underground atomic bomb tests. In counties to the north and east, water surges up in springs, deer and cattle graze on the sweet grass and alfalfa farmers bring in four harvests per year. Las Vegas covets their water. It has a plan for a $7 billion system of pumps and pipes to bring it to them. It has lined up an expensive team of lobbyists, lawyers and Washington politicians to push it through. It has even bought out a whole county of farmers. But even its own hydro-geologists say that it will turn the northern counties where the water is into an Owens Valley, a once-fertile region of farms and a lake in central California that was sucked dry by Los Angeles. Billowing clouds of dust loaded with arsenic blew from there over the southern part of the state. Los Angeles aspired to be some kind of Connecticut suburb in the sun. In this it was in denial about water in the way many other parts of the world are. Las Vegas is not so much in denial as in defiance. It consumes more water per person per day than anywhere else in America. Around its casinos it puts bays and canals and a fountain of a thousand jets that shoots water 240 feet into the air. Golf courses are spread throughout the valley. The science of ecology is thought a preserve of the weak. If things really get bad, however, a commentator said, they might ask people to take one less ice cube in their cocktails. The city, state and federal governments look on. Las Vegas may, like the profligate banks, be too big to be allowed to fail.

Time is defied as the natural elements are. A constant neutral, not quite locatable hour is aspired to in bars and casinos that have no natural light or exit signs or clocks, that pump in oxygen to keep you awake and that never close for even a minute. 'Party like there's no tomorrow.' The clock only begins to tick when the money runs out.

CINDI ROBINSON

Student

Money was always disappearing. Our allowance, Easter money, whatever our grandparents gave us. We'd put it away somewhere and whenever we went to look for it it'd be gone. We'd run to our mom and tell her and she'd say, 'The ghost took it.' So we had this rich, thieving ghost in the house. We'd tell people, 'All our money is going to the ghost!' But it was her.

I asked my dad how it was before. They were living in Torrance, California, a nice town near Los Angeles right on the ocean. When I was eight months old we moved to Vegas. My dad said life was normal before. They liked being married, having my sister and me. I saw the videos. They looked happy. But then it all fell apart. They divorced when I was five. My dad is on his fourth wife now.

This city just twisted my mother. She kept two cheque books, a real one and a fake one she showed my dad. He found out the truth when he went to the bank one day. After he left, the house was never clean, except on some family occasion day. We had dirty clothes, there wasn't enough food even though my dad sent child-support money. We kind of had to raise ourselves.

One day I came home from school and there was a notice on the door saying we had thirty days to get out. I went running in. 'There's nothing to worry about,' my mom said. 'It's a mistake. Everything's fine.' A week later there was a second notice on the door. I freaked. I called my dad and he must have done something because nothing else happened for weeks, until I was called out of chemistry class one day and found him in the hall. 'Your mother's lost the house,' he said. 'You've got two hours to pack.' There was a U-Haul already there by the time I got home. I was crying, screaming. That was my home just disappearing. She didn't even acknowledge me. It didn't faze her. It was like she lost a pair of earrings or something.

She started locking herself in her bedroom when I was six. We pounded on the door and screamed at her but she wouldn't answer. We were four, six and nine and we had to do everything around the house. We didn't know what she was doing in there. We still don't. There was just this silence. We all talked about her, trying to figure her out, put together the pieces of the puzzle. 'I don't know what happened to your mom,' my grandma'd say. 'She's not the same. She lies. She's not like my other kids.'

Around the time we lost the house she called me into her room and told me she had cancer. I was devastated. I was just on my way to church camp but felt I had to stay with her. When I told my dad he said not to believe it unless I had evidence. I got mad at him about that, but he was right, there was no sign of anything, of the disease or the treatment. She did the same thing with her knee, saying she had to have her meniscus replaced. She even hobbled around on crutches for two years. But there was no scar.

She stole money all the time. She stole from a woman whose house we were living in for a while and told the woman I did it. She stole all the money my sister had put away to get married. She never told anyone she was pregnant with my youngest brother until he was stillborn three months premature. She never bothered with any kind of ante-natal care. Nobody can figure it out. Why is she like this? Why doesn't she care about anybody? Why was she just this absence in our lives for all these years when we needed her so much? We can't even figure out what she does with the money. She still works. She gets paid well. My dad always sent child support. There's no tangible sign of what she spends it on. It all really got to me. I used to wrap my hair around my fingers and pull it out. I had bald spots all over my head. She's told so many lies I don't think she has a sense of reality any more. I think by now she actually believes she had cancer.

My sister says it has to be gambling or drugs. I don't know. Anything is possible. Lately her teeth are falling out. They started getting yellow and rotten about five years ago and now every time I see her another one is gone. She's only got about four or five left and they don't really look like teeth. Her breath reeks. She lost about thirty pounds in a month. Meth could do that, I guess. I don't really know about drugs. I never smelled anything.

I think if we stayed in California she might have been a liar but I don't think she would have been a thief. I don't think she'd have had anything to spend the money on. I know there are normal people here, normal families, but everyone in my family who's ever lived in Vegas has had problems. My dad drank a lot. He had a bad temper and went through marriage after marriage. The third one was an ex-showgirl who kept trying to get money from him and then ran away and wound up in an asylum. The present one is normal, but her previous husband cheated on her and had alcohol problems. Then there's my granddad. He's an obsessive gambler. When they go shopping he just sits and gambles the whole time and when my grandma comes back from her shopping she has to wait until he finishes. It's hard to find a healthy adult. The city just emanates this bad feeling. At least that's how I experience it. It invites people to develop their addictions and then they do it and throw everything away and are furious. It's a very angry city.

It's not easy to find healthy friends either. People get initiated early here. The girl I shared a dorm room with kept bringing in illegal substances. We had to evacuate once because a boy brought in a live grenade. I mean, where do you buy that? There was a murder at the bus stop beside the dorm, just outside my window. There was a boy I knew, Andrew, he was in the wrong place at the wrong time, around some kind of drug deal that went wrong. They shot him four times in the front yard of a house in Henderson, took him out to the desert – he was still breathing then – and beat him until he died. Then they buried him out near Primm and then drove his truck to Pahrump and burnt it. Girls become strippers, or worse, they hook up with men with drug problems who wind up in jail, they have babies they can't look after. One I knew was bragging on Facebook about how she can smoke pot while her baby's having a nap in the next room.

One boy in high school, he was a friend of mine, he overdosed. He didn't want to be around the bad any more. A girl at school was beaten by her father and now her younger brother's in court for beating his girlfriend. Another friend, she was in the Army Reserve, she was driving along Horizon Ridge three times over the limit and ran over an elderly couple and killed them. She's in jail for the next twenty-four years. The woman she killed was another friend's grandma. We're all linked together in this gigantic train wreck.

People are quick to deceive. They're skilled at it. They have second lives. All the temptation you could ever want is just down the road, not more than thirty minutes maximum away from wherever you live in this valley. People just haemorrhage their resources into it. Face is everything and it's expensive. You've got to have the best clothes just to get into the clubs. People have Audis and Lexuses when their children don't have enough to eat. They're thinking about how quick they can get to the next slot machine. This must be the world capital of debt.

I don't like the men here. Almost any guy I ever dated has cheated on me or been a drinker or used drugs or all three. I lived with one. He was just garbage. Abusive, mean. He cheated on me with a prostitute in northern Nevada. He's engaged to an ex-stripper now. I don't think I'm an obvious candidate for that kind of person. I mean, I always went to church, I'm not a party animal, I'm very straight. The city seems to draw that kind of man. Or turns them into it after they've been here a while. They're all about sex, getting it where they can and then lying to you. And why wouldn't they? You could be a little five-year-old boy sitting in the back of your family car driving down I-15 and see from all the billboards that it's all right to pay a girl to get naked for you. There's nothing private. It's all open and supposedly glamorous. I hate to watch them blowing all their family's money at a craps table, getting drunk and throwing up and stepping on you, hitting on you all the time in the most vile ways.

I have this friend, she went to Kansas. I may be stuck here at the University of Never Leaving Vegas, but she got away. She writes to me, 'Cindi, you wouldn't believe it. There are humans here! They don't binge, or at least not much. They smile, they're nice to you!'

I feel very insecure, like I'm just waiting for things to fall apart. I have a really nice boyfriend now. He's from New Jersey, a normal person. I love him but we get into fights all the time because I'm so suspicious. I have no reason to think he'll do anything to hurt me, but I keep looking for signs that he will. I go to a counsellor and feel well for about five hours and then go back to worrying. With both my ex-boyfriend and my mother I could ask them a question five times and get the same answer, and then the sixth time I'd get a different one. I live in dread of that changing answer.

It's difficult to live in a place you can't stand. It's normal to get bored. That could happen anywhere. But this is something else. This feels like some disease that's on your skin. They say, 'What happens in Vegas stays in Vegas.' But it's not true. I think it's going to stay with me for ever, wherever I go. I don't trust people. I'm full of anger towards the people who hurt me. I hate the way people behave, even the way it looks, all this lit up purple and red and gold and everything and then everywhere else this endless dull beige. I'd like to raise a family in a place where there's a community instead of all this transience and instability. I'd like to see grass and trees and animals and houses with different colours. I dream of having a dairy farm in Wisconsin. It wouldn't have to be there. Other places could work too. I've never been to a place that I didn't like, apart from this. Vegas makes you independent, I suppose. It forces it on you. We had to learn to cook and look after the house when we were small. It can make you morally aware. Obviously not everyone. But it worked like that for me. I'm very clear, I know exactly what I expect from other people and also from myself. I have strong willpower because it's constantly being tested here.

A lot of people didn't want me to talk to you. They don't want it out, especially if it's about them. But I'm glad to have the chance and I hope people will read it so they know what it costs to grow up in this place the world treats like a playground. This is a low, dirty place. We're right at the top in divorce, drugs, suicide and the sex trade and right at the bottom in education. We're the worst at anything of value. I don't look at the Strip and think, 'Oh, look at the pretty lights. I want to go and play.' I hate it. I want it to go away. It's just addictions and weakness that draw people here. We're the city that prides itself on moral corruption. It's like, 'We suck, come and visit us'. It's this Disneyland for malfunctioning grown-ups. They come and go, but the people who live here, they're stuck with it. They lose houses, jobs, husbands, wives, kids. The tourists don't see that. They don't see that the money they spend is going to hurt people, to perpetuate this illusion. It's on the way to being a wasteland and I hope it keeps going. So that's what I would ask of anyone who reads this – just don't come here.

On 18 May 2013 **Cindi Robinson** married Dominick Vocaturo, the boyfriend from New Jersey she refers to in her interview. The following day she graduated from UNLV with a degree in communications, carrying with her a $37,000 debt for her education. The next day she lost her job and spent nearly a year unemployed. She worked for a time at Nevada State College, but then she and her husband decided finally to find a way out of Las Vegas. She got a job at the University of Houston and once she has established residency in Texas plans to begin working on a master's degree in forensic anthropology. Her sister is employed as a photographer at the San Diego Zoo. Her brother still lives with their mother, whose health continues to deteriorate. No one as yet knows for certain what she does behind the locked door of her bedroom.

CHILDHOOD

At Treasure Island you can see actors playing pirates battling sirens in bustiers on a galleon in a large tank. A fifty-four foot high simulated rock volcano sizzles and flames and booms in front of the Mirage. The Star Trek Experience at the Hilton has closed, but there are singing gondoliers at the Venetian, waiters in togas at Caesars Palace, a pharaoh's tomb at the Luxor and drawbridge and towers at the Excalibur. There are sharks and tigers and lions behind glass. There are magic shows and acrobats and artists of the trapeze. You can whirl in a roller-coaster around the skyscrapers of New York New York or in the Adventuredome inside Circus Circus or you can be shot to the top of the Stratosphere and then freefall back again. At the Palms you can have your own bowling alley or basketball court in your room. If you step inside any of these places you can play slot machines that have dragons or wolves or leprechauns where the fruit used to be. You might even hear the old cartoon Chipmunks singing when it is time for a double jackpot.

Almost all the people you see engaging with these features are adults.

I wondered about this when I saw it. Why do so many people seek such ways to pass their time? Among the oldest of human rituals are puberty rites, in which young men and women are pierced, scarred, tattooed, circumcised, taken on hunts and vision quests and initiated into the secrets of the tribe. The rituals remind them that if they are old enough to produce a child they can no longer be children themselves. The rites are lines of demarcation. They have to be able to maintain and protect another life. They have to be accountable. In Ghana, young women are sequestered with their elders who tell them of children and men and their new status as women. The taking of a new name is often part of the ritual. This is the case with the Catholic ceremony of confirmation. The intention is to bring about the transformation described by Paul in a letter to the Corinthians: 'When I was a child, I spake as a child, I understood as a child, I thought as a child: but when I became a man I put away childish things.'

Las Vegas tells you that you need not do this, at least for as long as you are there. It spreads its bets. It offers you both a child's theme park and an adult playground. It can give you the toys and games and rides you knew from childhood or missed out on because they weren't invented yet. Then you can go somewhere else and drink with no closing time, make a mess, watch people take their clothes off, indulge, fantasize something and get others to act it out for you. In all cases the message is the same: you have a refuge — no one will ask you to clean up or scold you or tell on you, for what happens in Vegas, stays in Vegas. It has a unique pull because no other place in the world is devoted, as it is, entirely to this psychological relief. It is the siren that says, 'Go on, you deserve it. No one will know.'

'I hate Disneyland,' said Tom Waits. 'It primes our kids for Vegas.'

KENNETH PATRICK
(FORMERLY KENNETH BAKER)

Businessman

'There it is,' said my great-grandmother. She was talking about the Strip, glowing in the night. 'The jewel box.'

My story starts in Reno, though, rather than Vegas. My grandfather was the mayor there. Later he used to drive around the Southwest with my grandmother selling things out of his RV – car parts, belt buckles he'd made from melted down Liberty silver dollars. But to me he was always the mayor, 'The Father', the one who looked after people. He was a nice man, a jolly man. He was also a violent drunk. Everybody in my family was a drunk at some point.

My father was the mayor's son and my mother was a beauty queen. A perfect match. Part of my childhood consciousness was knowing that my dad could never get into trouble. He could get drunk and crash cars and it would be taken care of because of who he was.

We came down to Vegas when I was two because my dad wanted to get involved in politics. I remember stuffing envelopes for Harry Reid's failed mayoral campaign, getting into matching bell-bottomed jumpsuits with my sister and putting political stickers on people at a picnic. We were in commercials. Our business was promoting other people. My father was a rageful man who was rarely at home. I was terrified of him when he was sober and it was worse when he was drunk. He'd wander off for periods or arrive late and drunk and black out, then take the kids apart when he woke up before turning on the adults. I remember waking up to a broken chair. He slept with other women. I loathed and feared him and at the same time craved his attention.

I think I started drinking not long after I learned to walk. I'd be on beer runs back and forth from the kitchen for my father and drink what was left in the cans. I got to be a passed-out drunk when I was eight. We drove out to Ely in the middle of the state for a Basque festival. The men were all drinking and my dad thought it would be fun to put the kids in a drinking contest. We drank port wine out of goatskin bota bags. They tied beach towels around our necks as bibs. You know, never mind the kid, just preserve the shirt. I was the last man standing, as it were. I beat out a twelve-year-old. I was proud of that. Then I passed out. When I came to I was in a bed in a little motel called the Idle Inn with a cold cloth on my head being looked after by an old woman who had just two teeth. When she left the room to get more water for the cloth I saw a can of beer on the bedside table. I thought, What would my dad do? So I drank it. I had to spit out a cigarette butt that had been left in it.

My parents divorced when I was seven. My mother had been married to a tyrant for eleven years, she was thirty and single, it was Vegas and 1972 and the party was on. It was a party before that and it's still a party now and it's not for kids. I wish I didn't grow up here. I wish I grew up in a place where the parents were at home at weekends and you all did things together and they looked after you. They keep trying to think up new features to lure families here. Most of us say, 'Please don't.' There are few things more disgusting than a family going through a casino with a stroller. I wound up having the kind of childhood many Vegas kids have. My dad had disappeared and now my mom started doing it. She worked swing shift and the graveyard shift in a cashier's cage in a casino. She'd be out in the bars a lot and hungover when she was home. That left us to our own devices. I was doing the laundry, organizing the housework, paying the paperboy, writing letters to teachers if my sister was sick – all by the time I was eight. She brought men home one after the other. My sister was furious. She'd make all sorts of noise to disturb them, running the vacuum, banging into my mother's bedroom door. But I was fascinated. I used to sit there on the edge of my seat like it was the most exciting kind of theatre, just waiting to see who would come out.

I knew I was gay by the time I was four. My dad had a friend named Larry who was just 5'1", just an adorable guy. He was so tiny he seemed closer to our world than theirs. I had a crush on him. He used to joke with my sister, 'You and me, babe, just give it twenty-five years and we'll be a couple.' That hurt. I thought, But what about me? He had dark hair, dark skin. That's the type I've been chasing ever since.

My mom did guys who could make her life easier. In time she and I both went after casino executives, Vegas aristocracy, the kind of men who had cell phones before anyone else. She still romanticizes the era of the boys from Kansas City running the Tropicana, the pre-corporation days when the city was small and she felt special and safe because she worked for Benny Binion. There were low points, undoubtedly. When I was seventeen she called me from a hotel. She'd met a couple of men in a bar and spent some time in a room with them, then couldn't remember where she'd left her car. She was bawling and bawling, saying, 'I can't believe I had to call my son.' I just drove her home. I hardly noticed.

She and her friends had this hierarchy and swore they'd never date casino dealers – 'squealers', they called them, guys who'd come into town on a motorcycle with five hundred bucks chasing the dream, then blow it all and have to get a job dealing blackjack. But she didn't keep her word. She had one guy, black Irish, very good-looking, who was a dealer at the Dunes. That was the place for serious cash then. He was so terrified of losing his job that he'd wear ladies' cologne and play gay because the pit boss was gay. He was a heroin addict and a drunk and a Vietnam vet, completely off his rocker. He'd get up in the night and pee in the corner and then go back to sleep. He'd show us the scars on his back from bullet wounds and before and after photographs of villages they'd wasted. He was very sexually present. He'd get a notion and take my mother into her room. I'd hear things coming out of there a boy shouldn't hear. It drove my great-grandmother out of the house, but it intrigued me. I thought he knew things. I started to fantasize about him. But before I did anything about it I went out and found it elsewhere. That would have been too weird.

Eventually my mom married an alcoholic, heavy cocaine-using, gambling-addicted philanderer who was ten years younger than her. He was also homophobic. It took her years to tell him about me. Still, through it all she kept us together. Out of all the people I knew whose parents were divorced we were the only ones to stay in the same house from kindergarten through high school.

They found I had a high IQ when I was a kid and I imagined this made my teachers afraid of me. I believed myself exempted from homework. From fourteen years old I was out chasing drink and men. Two years later I was just 5'4", 110 lbs. and looked about ten. I was a flaming queen because that was the only kind of gay man I saw on television in the seventies. I thought that was what you had to do. It was a great relief when I picked up a construction worker with dirty nails and realized it was all right to be masculine. I'd go into the men's room at J.C. Penney's in the Boulevard Mall. Anyone who went in there could get what he wanted for sure. I turned tricks, blew guys for twenty bucks in the back arcades of adult bookstores to get enough money to buy clothes to attract more important people. I had to sneak in on my hands and knees because I was underage.

I finally got my own hotel executive. He was head of house-keeping at Caesars. His name was Frank. He was thirty-two, I was halfway through high school. I dressed to impress him. I had paper routes, worked in the school cafeteria, sold person-alized Christmas cards door-to-door and anything else a boy could sell at the time. I saved $400 and spent it all on one outfit.

It drove my mom nuts. I did that kind of thing for decades. Years later I was living in the Palms Apartments on Sahara in one those old showgirl places with enormous closets. I had $30,000 worth of clothes in there and half of them still had their price tags on. It made me so sad. For Frank I'd put on my new cashmere sweater and Florsheim shoes. He'd pick me up, take me to his place, get me drunk, have sex with me and when I'd wake up he'd get me drunk again and pass me around to his friends. He'd do my homework for me so we'd have more time. Frank was the kind of guy who would get to know your parents so he could have better access. He got me a job in a bank. He liked his boys to work. I kept leaving him because he kept fucking boys younger than me. He'd get older but they always stayed sixteen. He had boys all over the place and I'd see him with them, but that didn't stop him from being insanely jealous. I'd been in a bar called the Clown's Den on Boulder Highway and he thought I'd taken someone from there back to an apartment I had when I was seventeen. I was in my pyjamas and about to go to bed when he smashed through a glass door, started screaming 'Where is he?', beat me all around the face and nearly choked me to death. The neighbours called the cops and he ran off. A cop asked me, 'Did you know your attacker?' 'Yes,' I said. 'He's a former boyfriend.' He closed his notebook and walked. It was just two fags beating each other up. That's another reason to hate this city.

There was an eerie little epilogue to the Frank story. When I was twenty-seven and hadn't heard from him in many years he called me. He'd left Vegas and was in Florida working for the government on border patrol. He'd run my social security number through the system and got my contact details. 'I just want you to know I'm keeping an eye on you,' he said.

I wanted to be one of the people who strode through casinos, the kind executives paid attention to. I wanted to have the right watch, the right car, the right suit. I wanted people to see I had those things and to be subservient to me. Then I'd know what it really felt like. I used to stand in front of Caesars watching the tourists from Ohio photographing the glitterati pulling up in their Lotuses. I'd think, I want to be that guy. I want them to take pictures of *me*. Needless to say I had no plans to be one of the people who cleans their toilets. It's a dream factory, the only place in America other than Hollywood where people arrive thinking their lives can transform in a single instant. And there's not a single thing in the world that can let you know this has happened other than money.

I was highly susceptible to rejection when I was small. I expected to be forgotten and left. I remember my mother telling me that my father was coming to visit. I was very excited and nervous. I had a bath, got dressed up, shined my shoes and then sat in a chair for four hours. He'd forgotten. By the time my mom got home I was catatonic. But Vegas will harden you. I felt constantly rejected by what the city stood for and demanded and finally you find a way to just live with it. Maybe that's why I'm such a good salesman now. Reject me all week, I don't care. Call your friends and they can do it too. I learned early.

This is a city that for a long time had a single industry that got right into the neighbourhoods and houses. My grandmother made her own roulette wheel for the house. We played blackjack at home all my life. It's a special industry. It's not like

Detroit. It plays with the mind, throws up glamorous images. There's so much sadness and desolation and anger here. I brought a Mexican boyfriend here once and asked him what he thought. 'Everyone's in a hurry and everyone's angry,' he said. This is a city populated by a vast army of servers. They're opening doors, cleaning rooms, running cocktails and bringing towels for people who've left their manners at home, who are pissed off because they've lost their whole bankroll on their first night in town or who are acting like assholes because they've won a few grand at a craps table. A whole shift of waitresses walked off because some basketball players who were here for an event thought it was fine to put their hands up the girls' skirts. The people here are absorbing this day in and day out. The deal here is that you crumble or you stand. You go for the brass ring. I saw the pretty girls getting picked off at high school. They're all plastic surgery and fake boobs now, but once they were teenagers with men two or three times their age who got them before boys their own age could. This is a city of eighteen-year-old girls and fifty-year-old men. I was one myself, only I was a boy. I was a pretty boy, and tiny, and willing. A lot of the time it all goes wrong and they become strippers. They're good people, but it takes a part of their soul. They take drugs. They don't want to be present to observe what they've become. Everybody knows you can come here and money will get you what you want. The city promotes itself on that. Frank had a fourteen-year-old boyfriend named Glenn. He was long and lanky, just beautiful. He looked like Julie Andrews when he was in drag. He'd be walking around with thousands of dollars in his pocket because a Saudi prince was crazy about him. The prince would fly in, tip the bell captain at Caesars to find Glenn and then pay him $5,000 to spend the weekend with him. The bell captain at Caesars will get you anything you want. Triplets with green eyes? Give him five minutes.

Of course love doesn't come into it. I never really knew what it was. Johns would say to me, 'I love you, I love you.' I didn't know what they were talking about. I was honest with them. 'Well, I don't love you,' I'd say. But it wasn't just the johns. I've only just realized, with a truly great sadness I have to say, that I've never loved anybody, outside the strange and complicated love I feel for my family. I've never felt the hurt you have to feel.

I've had sex with thousands of men. I'd get smashed, pick up a man and have sex with him, then go out and do it all again, maybe three or four times in a night. Every day I'd drink a fifth of Jack and a six-pack of beer and snort coke. I kept booze in my office desk drawer. I'd go out with friends and drift, something my dad used to do. No one knew what happened to me. I'd end up in other states not knowing how I'd got there. I kept changing identities, as alcoholics do. Fail in one, pick up another. I even got married. She had more coke than I did because she had more money and I thought it'd be fun. I sold drugs – coke, crystal meth, pot, ludes, valium – and consumed them all. I've been in jail, been put in psychiatric wards. I'd think about how the people in Reno had liked my grandfather enough to elect him and I'm a fucking drug dealer. I don't know how I look like I do. All the meth heads I've ever seen have no teeth.

I found out I had AIDS in 1986, a month before I turned twenty-one. I probably got it during the Frank years. I didn't really address it until 1999. When I took the pills my cell count went up and my viral load went down and the doctors were happy, but I felt so bad with nausea and insomnia that I couldn't go to work. I've thrown away three prescriptions of AZT. Everyone I knew who took it has died. I have no medical answer to the question as to how I have survived. I drink water, try to eat well and get enough sleep. I have also refused to be categorized by AIDS, gay or even male. I'm just kennybaker, just that, a single word that's me and only me. I like to hear people say it that way. In my family we have a lot of liabilities – alcoholism, chronic relationship breakdown, suicide. My mom's mom was a model until she was forty-two and then obese and dead of sclerosis at forty-six. My grandfather the mayor both hanged himself and shot himself in the temple. He wasn't kidding. He'd been given some diagnosis of diabetes and schizophrenia that made him feel he'd be dependent on his wife and therefore 'not a man' and left her a note telling her not to worry about the cost of the gun because he'd hocked a pair of boots to pay for it. We're a catalogue of people who can't see past our noses. But we also tend to have unusual longevity. I can remember being with my great-great-grandmother and she was born in something like 1885. So I have that on my side. Maybe too the city has helped me to get through. Vegas will teach you how to be alone, how to be tough and how to survive, if you let it. In fact, just saying that makes me see it in a new light. It was good for something.

I'd say 2005 was our first year of puberty. That's when the convention business overtook gambling in revenue generation. Now we're teenagers and teenagers are not nice people. Maybe in a hundred years we'll be wonderful. There are efforts to diversify the economy, develop medical services in a Mayo

Clinic kind of way, build a symphony hall. I'd like to see the healing arts brought here. So far they've tended not to cross the California border. We certainly need them.

All of us, my father, my mother, my sister and me, are recovering alcoholics. My dad got there first and my mom last. When she was first thinking of going to the Twelve-Step meetings she asked, 'Can I drink in between? Can I do the steps I want?' Then when they went around the room and introduced themselves and said they were alcoholics, she just said, 'I'm here with my son.' Finally she caved in and admitted it. I've been sober for thirteen years. I credit the programme I was in and am still in with any spiritual quality, introspection or charitable impulses I possess. After being a drug dealer and a prostitute I've become a person I don't at all mind spending time with. I feel well. The huge liver I had is now half the size. I run marathons with my sister. We've completed two so far. You have to write on the back of your number bib about any serious medical conditions you might have and of course I wrote AIDS. When my sister saw it she broke down and cried. 'Who'd have thought you'd live to see this?' she said.

When I was a kid Frank snuck me the key to Cher's suite in the Fantasy Tower at Caesars. They'd designed it for her to her specifications. I walked around with my mouth open. I could hardly breathe. It had a thirty-two person Jacuzzi surrounded by windows that looked down on the Strip. Can it possibly get better than this? I thought. Now all I want is some lush grass, a stream to sit by, and silence.

The year after this interview, **Kenneth Patrick** (then still Kenneth Baker) completed a 23-kilometre foot race in Cambodia. Standard and endurance marathon running had come to be at the heart of his quest for spiritual and physical health. Most of the members of his immediate family continue not to drink, but he is the only one who remains in a recovery programme. Because of what he senses to be a lack of self-care and introspection on their part, he is more distant from them at times. He moved to southern California, having cut most of his professional ties to Las Vegas, and works in real estate and life coaching. In 2015 he got caught in a flood, which gave rise to an infection directly related to HIV. He nearly died. At the time of writing he is back to eighty per cent capacity and has returned to training for long-distance running. One of the things that came out of his near-encounter with death was his decision to change his name to Kenneth Patrick.

The mother of excess is not joy
but joylessness.

Friedrich Nietzsche

EPILOGUE

We packed our lamps and books and sheets and sent them home. We gave our car to our landlady's church, said good-bye and flew out. As we rose over the valley the sun overwhelmed the lights of the Strip and blanched the land. The air rippled in the heat. Again that feeling that the place was not entirely there, that it was vanishing as I looked at it. The voices of the ten children of Las Vegas were on a recording machine in a bag under my seat.

We came home to Torun, a medieval walled Polish city on the Vistula River. It was late spring. I took the recording machine into our garden and began to transcribe what had been said. Bees and butterflies moved among the flowers. I heard the whine of an electrical saw from a carpenter's workshop, birdsong, the table of my neighbour being laid for lunch, speech, radios, laughter, invective, the passing of car tyres over the cobbled street. A student up in a garret played Jean Michel Jarre. I saw the worn leather briefcase of a passing elderly man through the slats of our wooden fence. Had he had this briefcase long? I wondered. Did it belong to his grandfather? It may have been older than anything I had seen in Las Vegas. The voices played on the machine and I wrote down what they said. I remembered the empty sidewalks in Las Vegas, the huge vehicles that looked so anonymous and predatory, like military drones, the sense of a general turning away. Here the streets were cacophonous. People leaned out of their windows to watch the pageant. The little vehicles passing on the road were the size of a Hummer's door. Everything was there to see, within reach, immediate. The voices on the machine were also like that.

The first person to suggest to me that I write about Las Vegas was the writer Eric Schlosser. 'You have in crystallized form there all the ways we've gone wrong,' he said. I wasn't sure what he meant then. I hadn't been there long enough, perhaps. I felt as F.B.I. agent Joe Yablonsky did when he was sent to Las Vegas. 'One of the first responses I had was, Is this really part of the United States?'

I never really did write about it in the sense that Eric meant, including here in this book, where the job is to provide a venue for those who have more authority than I, but I came to see better his point and, as perhaps Agent Yablonsky also eventually saw, that Las Vegas is not a freak but is, instead, deeply integrated with the rest of the country, and the world beyond. It is symptom, mirror, metaphor. It reads human wishes and incarnates them on the desert floor. Is it not the intention of its most famous promotional slogan 'What happens in Vegas, stays in Vegas' to send waves of excitement and moral relief coursing through the psyche? Is this not recognizable to all of us? The city's story is more the story of these secret human wishes than it is of its ecology or industries or its sequence of mayors.

America embarked on one of its epochal changes at the beginning of the 1980s and as the change moved forward the country came increasingly to resemble Las Vegas. Financial services for the first time surpassed manufacturing in their share of the gross domestic product. New trading devices, both fantastical and inscrutable, were invented. Vast leveraging took place. Debt itself was made into a tradable security, becoming a kind of ball on a roulette wheel and absolving the original creditor of any responsibility to collect. The cautious, sober bankers of my childhood were transformed into the bravado high rollers of the 1990s and 2000s, who played the markets during the week and took their rest and recreation in Las Vegas. They had nicknames, like the notorious London Whale whose vast bets cost J.P. Morgan $6 billion. Profits were skimmed, junk unloaded, bonuses taken. A cult of ostentatious wealth developed. Cocaine, the drug of status enhancement, boomed. Sensation, play and fantasy too went into the ascendant. Adults went to work on motorized skateboards. Planes, cars, houses and even people were conceptualized as toys. In a time of cheap production businesses concentrated on creating demand rather than on just serving it. Advertising became tailor-made. Addictions – to games, beauty products, pornography, phones, gossip, processed food – created the paths to profit. Scientists and psychologists and medical doctors helped create the recipes. Now became the time in which people dwelt, in cathartic psychotherapies or pills that offered instant relief, in TV evangelisms that sold salvation, and in mass consumption on credit. It was an all-out binge and it needed money to keep it spinning, money that was becoming increasingly fictional. Government, corporate and personal debt ballooned. There wasn't the collateral. The system grew hotter as it spiralled upwards. No one wanted it to end, but it finally did.

The era of debt was succeeded by the era of default. There had been a time of soaring appetites and the invention of new ways to gratify them; there was a time of surfeit, and after that there was a time when a morbid kind of hangover spread over the land. It had happened before. Wild borrowings and speculation preceded the falls of Hapsburg Spain, the Dutch and the British and also the 1929 crash. The same Greek civilization which had invented philosophy and science and politics turned to Epicureanism and Cynicism and a belief in Fortune and Chance when invading Macedonian armies took away their homes.

What happens in Vegas happens above all to those holding the lowest status there, the residents. I used to wonder at the large number of cars in the Strip parking garages, the hordes playing slots in the neighbourhood casinos. Could there be so many tourists with old, dusty cars? Why would they come out to a casino on Boulder Highway, or in Henderson? It was, of course, the city's citizens, people who finished their shifts at one casino and paid in their wages to another. A survey conducted in Canada showed that the seventy-five per cent of casino customers who only play occasionally account for just four per cent of revenue. The rest comes from high rollers and the hooked, and many of the latter are likely to be local citizens.

Las Vegas is a constantly evolving experiment. It creates templates. It is the world expert at what it does. It sometimes seemed to me like a giant scanning device looking for insecurity and greed and a propensity for fantasy. It reaches out into the wide world looking for marks. On a London tube I saw an ad with an image of the Strip superimposed with the text 'Visit a Place Where Your Accent Is an Aphrodisiac. What Happens Here, Stays Here. Go to www.VisitLasVegas.co.uk and Plan a

Holiday You Won't Write Home About.' The more corporate it has become the more finely calibrated its sensors. It looks for those who want to return to childhood, those who seek solutions in a stroke of luck, those who dream of having their secret desires served up to them without censure. They are everywhere to be found. Their migration to Las Vegas was like that of other great American migrations to oil fields and fruit farms and streams running with gold. Some came to walk in the sun and pass their time in supervised play, others to get lucky. Most came for the easy money to be got from low-skill jobs. They found a place that serves and stimulates around the clock, in which every minute is filled, where everyone, even the solitary slot player on Boulder Highway, is made to feel the centre of their universe, and yet it is a place where no one is the author of their own entertainment. No one may like to think about it, but they know that you must play by the house rules and with the house odds. When the math runs true and the money runs out and you cannot get it back you are sent away. Then you may feel bad. And when people feel bad, many do as Nevada Stupak's father did. They medicate. Adrenaline and anaesthesia are the twin poles between which the bit players in this city pass.

I met many people in Las Vegas who did not live this way. They were healthy, solvent. They kept their homes and attended to their children. But the vacant houses, the halted developments, the golf courses gone to seed and the default figures pointed to a trend. The desert was creeping in at the edges. It erupted sometimes in the heart of the city. It seemed to me that the hangover aura, the isolation, furtiveness, anxiety and boredom were all unmistakeable. Anger broke out in the roads. I had never been anywhere where such qualities were so salient in the atmosphere of a city. Las Vegas leads the nation in suicides, teenage drug use, drunk-driving arrests, household bankruptcy, divorce and high school dropout rates. Alcohol, smoking both active and passive, epidemic dependencies on both illegal and prescribed drugs, poor healthcare and social services resulting from the low-tax regime, stress from debt, shame and despair have conspired to place Las Vegas very near the bottom of life-expectancy tables. A construction worker prematurely aged by twenty years declared, 'It is the city itself that is killing me.' The great sources of the city's revenue weigh heavily on its citizens. This is a secret about which it strives to remain in denial.

The people who speak in this book don't want to feel that way or to live like that. They've grown up with a sickness that is general and chronic, they've lived in the shadows of a city of lights, as Shelby Sullivan said. The colonized tend to know their colonizers far better than the other way around and it is the same, it would seem, with the people in this book and their city. They've watched it since they could first perceive and think. They are its witnesses. There has been very little to distract them from contemplating its weaknesses and its strengths. They are down at the bottom of a chain along with their fellow citizens and families, being grazed upon for profit. They try to find ways to survive. They look for the authentic, for meaning, for an adulthood where there is a reckoning for what you do and for some kind of future beyond the insistent, insatiable and never ending Now. They look for some sign of kindness. They suffer, they struggle, try to learn. They have parents who have gone beyond excess into helplessness. In most cases what they learn from them will only harm them, except in a cautionary way, for they live in houses where nature has been reversed, where the child, early in life, became carer and custodian for the parent.

I don't know what Las Vegas should do. It is unlikely to go away. Banning the things that have built it won't solve the yearning for them. Forty-one million people visit every year. More than two million live and make their incomes there. Some have happy memories. They like it the way it is. But these stories can't be made to go away either. They are not unique, as any one of their authors can tell you. They are an unshiftable part of the city. If they had happened in Gary, Indiana or Birmingham in England they would be sad, a grim part of the fabric of urban life. But these stories happened not only in Las Vegas, but because of the way it conceives of and sells itself and because of the people who come to buy what it offers.

In our garden I made their voices into texts. These texts seemed to me like small bombs. Steve Pyke and I put a few of them into a proposal. We sent it out to newspapers and magazines and book publishers and waited. We thought we'd be taking our pick. But that's not what happened. Most didn't answer. Others turned it down. It was too local, or too bleak. Someone at Vanity Fair said they might consider it if a celebrity were involved. That's what they actually said.

This surprised me. It still does. I thought that anyone reading these stories would react as I had in the classroom, that they would be stunned there was such a place, a strange and unique place so celebrated for its riches and glamour that had yet bequeathed to its own children lives that no one deserved to live. I thought the stories were for everyone because the place had been made in the image of what it believed all of us wanted. It seemed to me that what they described was a very unusual emergency. They were victims not of war or pestilence or sexual predators or economic breakdown or their own foibles, but rather of a peculiar version of fun. To be with them had nothing of bleakness about it. They were sharp, funny, eloquent. They struggled for, and in large part attained, transcendence. They arrived one by one at our home by the golf course. Their words came down on me as we sat at our table through the hours. They'd get up then, unaccountably say 'thank you' and go. If they were students they'd likely go to some job at a discount store or casino or fast-food place, and then to school again in the morning. It cost them sometimes to say what they did. And they took some risk, for people close to them may come to hate them for it. They knew that and did it anyway. They would like to be heard, and they hope, I think, for something more than pity.

ACKNOWLEDGEMENTS

I'd like to thank the Black Mountain Institute in Las Vegas for giving me the time and the setting to develop this. Tom and Mary Gallagher sponsored my fellowship there and became friends. Our landlady, Sheila Siino, was a warm and generous presence through the whole of our time there. Judith Nies, also a Black Mountain fellow, told me of the links between the lights of Las Vegas and the coal mines on Navajo land. Her book Unreal City deals with this. Matthew O'Brien, author of Beneath the Neon and My Week at the Blue Angel, provided valuable introductions. Steve Pyke immediately came out to Las Vegas when I told him about these stories and, with his now wife, Nic Kaczorowski, produced the portraits here. My agent David Godwin has been behind this book since he first read it. I'm grateful to Fong Hoe Fang and his Ethos Books in Singapore, and to John Mitchison and Rachael Kerr of Unbound, who helped rescue another book of mine twenty years ago, along with everyone else I worked with at Unbound. I am especially grateful to all the friends and people unknown to me who made the pledges that have enabled the book's publication. Black Mountain, the Gallaghers and Mark Knopfler made particularly splendid contributions. We may not have got there without them. I won't thank the interview subjects for they are as much the authors of this book as I am.

Unbound is a new kind of publishing house. Our books are funded directly by readers. This was a very popular idea during the late eighteenth and early nineteenth centuries. Now we have revived it for the internet age. It allows authors to write the books they really want to write and readers to support the writing they would most like to see published.

The names listed below are of readers who have pledged their support and made this book happen. If you'd like to join them, visit: www.unbound.co.uk.

Paul Austin
Stuart Borthwick
Steve Brierly
Sonia Brock
Julia Buckley
Fay Capstick
Victoria Chang
Melanie Chrysostomou
Martin Colthorpe
Philip Connor
John Crawford
Seamus Crowe
Dave (hedgecutter.com)
Bex Dawkins
Stu Dearnley
John Delaney
Nick Drake
Sean Dromgoole
Joseph Figueira
Andrew Fitzsimons
Tom Gallagher
Amro Gebreel
Sean Golden
Robert Gregory
Judith Griffith

Dana Gynther
Sean Harkin
Mary M Hart
John Hawkins
Lamar Herrin
Henry Jackman
Marjorie Johns
John Kearns
Dan Kieran
Steven King
Mark Knopfler
Aditya Kripalani
Joseph Langdon
Kristin Lockhart
Anthony Lott
Tony Lundon
Joe Mackin
Adrian McBride
Gary McKeone
David McRedmond
Grant Millar
Greg Blake Miller
John Mitchinson
Ken Monaghan
Nancy Morris

Shivanjani Naidu
Carlo Navato
Georgia Odd
Sarah Patmore
Luisa Plaja
Justin Pollard
Rachel Ramoni
The Beverly Rogers,
  Carol C. Harter
  Black Mountain
  Institute
Richard Romano
Andrew Schwab
Joshua Shenk
Sheila Siino
Jeff Skinner
Craig Vaughton
Padma Viswanathan
Simon Walden
Philip Watson
Hannah Whelan
Angelique Winston
Clive Winters
Linda Youdelis